BEYOND LIFE

BEYOND LIFE

THE GHOST CHRONICLES!

Stories Written By:

Daniel Norvell & Sandra Wells

authorHOUSE®

AuthorHouse™
1663 Liberty Drive
Bloomington, IN 47403
www.authorhouse.com
Phone: 1-800-839-8640

First published by AuthorHouse   09/02/2011

ISBN: 978-1-4567-9397-5 (sc)
ISBN: 978-1-4567-9396-8 (hc)
ISBN: 978-1-4567-9395-1 (ebk)

Library of Congress Control Number: 2011915098

Printed in the United States of America

Contents

Dedication

This book is dedicated to our family and friends who without their love and support this project would not have come to pass

Introduction

Being a paranormal investigator I have continually tried to come up with different theories on ghosts. What are their stories? How do they react to different situations. When I began to sit down and write my stories I had to go back over many of the different theories I had thought about over the 25 yrs of doing this research into the afterlife. Then I pulled from those idea's as to what it would be like to be a ghost, what they must endure, how sad many of them must feel by being stuck in a world that no longer needs them. Once I realized and put myself into their shoes so to speak the stories came easily to relay to you our readers. All of my characters, and places are completely fictional but are loosely based on many interactions I have experienced over the years in either communication or contact with all types of ghosts. I did my best to help you the reader be able to visualize the afterlife for these ghosts.

Sandy Wells

Have you ever been sitting up by yourself late at night, and wondered if you are being watched? What is it that is watching? What is it that they are observing? Do they observe our deepest darkest secrets? Do they observe the evil that we do? These are a few ideas that came to me as I wrote these stories, and it is what I have conveyed to you, the reader. I have a belief that at times, truth is stranger than fiction, and these stories are fictional ideas from my mind. I do want you all to think about this, what if it isn't?

Daniel Norvell

For God And Country

Written By: Daniel Norvell

Section One

For God And Country

I was 20 years old when that cannonball hit me in the chest. When I signed up, I never thought I would die in the war. I always hoped that I would someday meet President Lincoln and shake his hand. I respected the man and never gave a second thought to serving in the Union Army.

I was Corporal Jeremiah Deakins, Union Soldier, and I vividly remember the day I died.

It was a warm, sunny fall afternoon. I was moving my men to another position on the battlefield when I lost my life. I heard the cannon blast just about the time the ball ripped a hole through my chest. Death came very quickly for me; I hardly had time to feel any pain.

I remember lying on my back, or what was left of it, and I turned my head to the side and gasped my last breath. As I stared into the eyes of one of my men, whom had also been killed, I noticed a bright light on the hillside. Instantly, I was on my feet and walking toward this brilliant light with about 23 other men. I looked at the other men walking with me. There was yelling and confusion, cannon fire and gunfire all around us. I remember looking back at my lifeless body and thinking, "Well, at least Momma will have something to bury."

I continued toward the light along with both Union and Reb soldiers. Most of the fellas walked right into the light, but one of the Rebs and I decided not to go. I have regretted that decision a few times since but, because of it, I've observed many things come to pass throughout the history of this nation.

The Reb looked at me. "Hey Yank, what the hell happened to us?"

"Well Reb, I think we died. I think the war is over for you and me."

We sat on the hillside, that Reb and I, and watched the battle until it was over. There were many groans and a lot of smoke in the air. Death was all around us. There were more soldiers walking toward the hillside and they just seemed to disappear into nowhere. I never saw them again. Suddenly, that Reb jumped to his feet and took off running.

He caught up with some of the men walking toward the hillside and I never saw him again. I decided that I would make my way to our nation's capitol. I really had no idea what my existence would consist of, but I wanted to walk on the lawn of the White House before I moved on to meet our Lord. I had no idea what I would see, but I felt the need to travel to Washington and at least gaze upon the face of the man I admired the most.

I was not sorry I had lost my life for my nation and even if he couldn't hear me, I was going to tell President Lincoln that he had made the right choices. I would die for the man again if it was possible.

I walked for what seemed like weeks. I came into a clearing one night and there was a lot of commotion with men shouting and screaming. I walked into this small group of men as they were placing a rope around the neck of a young Negro. The young man was terrified.

"Sir, please . . . I was hungry. I'll work to pay for the meat I took. I'm going home to my family. Please don't kill me!"

His pleas fell on deaf ears. I ran into the group of men and tried to tell them to stop, but I couldn't do anything. They placed that man on a horse and tied the rope to a branch. They called him a thief and said, "For your crimes, you are sentenced to death by hanging. May God have mercy on your soul."

They slapped the horse and, when it bolted, the young man's neck snapped, leaving him dangling and still twitching. I hit my knees and shook my head. "Dear God, why? Why do men do such evil things to each other over the color of skin?"

It was the first time I had ever seen a man hang and I was sick to my stomach. I could not believe that I could still feel sickened by anything even though I was dead. "I am sorry young man. I wish I could have stopped them."

I felt a hand on my shoulder. "I know you would have, soldier." I turned and there, standing beside me, was the man these animals had just murdered.

"I was traveling home to see my Momma. I found some ham that had fallen off a horse and was eating it when they rode up. They hung me for a piece of ham."

"I'm sorry. I am so sorry. I lost my life trying to free your people."

"It's OK, soldier. I have to go now. Why don't you come with me?"

I looked into the man's eyes. "I cannot. I am going to Washington to gaze upon the President before I go anywhere else. I will get there before I go to be with our Lord." I wasn't sure why it was so important to me to go to Washington, but I was determined.

"Travel in peace, soldier. Thank you for your service for my people." I looked around and he was gone. All that was left was his body hanging from that tree. I sat down along the road with a heavy heart. I had just witnessed one of the cruelest acts ever. It would not be the last.

As I continued my journey to the nation's capitol, I passed a house early one morning and realized how nice it would be just to smell a home cooked meal. I made my way to the house and entered. I could smell bacon cooking.

I sure missed food and I missed a good horseback ride through the woods outside of the town I lived in. I was standing in the kitchen watching the woman of the house cook while her daughter helped.

The man of the house came down from upstairs and they sat and began to eat. I listened to the family talk and it made me miss my own family. I should have traveled to see my mother instead of going to the capitol, but something drew me there. I couldn't explain it.

There came a knock at the door and the man of the house answered it, inviting the caller in. I heard the man call to his wife in a trembling voice. I heard a scream and followed the sound.

The woman of the house was on her knees, sobbing loudly, and her husband was consoling her. There was a Union captain standing in the doorway. He had just advised them of their son's death in battle.

I left them to mourn in peace, saying a prayer for the family as I went. I remembered that my own mother had received similar news just months back and I wished that I had reconsidered my choice of joining the army after what I had just observed. I thought of how my little brother and three sisters might have reacted when they got the news of my passing. My father was proud that I chose to serve, but I knew he was apprehensive at the same time.

I would never know the pain of burying a son lost to battle and I didn't envy my family for the pain my death had caused. I continued my journey with a heavy heart.

I had been a young man with a long life ahead of me. I had promised to return and work for my father at his newspaper. I even left behind the girl I was to marry. What a fool I was to enter into war so blindly! I am proud to have served my country, and my President, but I may have made a mistake.

I spent the rest of that day reminding myself of the injustice I had observed when those men hung that young man for no good reason, and the heaviness seemed to subside.

It was a few nights later that I had made my way into a small town that reminded me of home. The streets were filled with people and I knew that it must be the Fourth of July. I made my way down the street and saw a man standing in the cemetery. He watched me as I walked by but he never spoke a word. I felt uneasy as I passed and I knew that I had just seen another dead man. He must not be able to leave his body in the cemetery or something, I thought.

I was glad I had walked away from my body back on that battlefield, although I wondered where it ended up. I thought of the times I had spent as a boy with my friends at the swimming hole and the things we all used to do together. But every time I think of that young man hanging from that tree, I do not regret the choice that I made.

I was standing outside of a house and a young man and woman were sitting on the porch. He was talking with her but I could not quite hear what was being discussed. All at once, the woman stood up and smacked the young man across his face. The young man got very mad, grabbed her by her hair, and dragged her around the back of the house. I followed them and saw that the man was on top of the woman. After he finished, he started to beat the woman in the face over and over. I ran over and tried to hit the man but it was no use. The man kept beating this young woman until I heard gurgling and I watched her take her last breaths.

I was outraged. Why didn't anyone hear this and come to her aid? There was celebrating going on and that was the cover this coward needed to carry out his act. The young man ran off and I followed. I was met at the gate by the man that was standing in the cemetery.

"Thank you for caring. I knew you would try to save my daughter, but I was sent here to bring her with me," he said.

"Daddy?" said a voice behind me. It was the young woman that I had just observed being beaten to death. The man placed his arm around her and they walked to the cemetery and disappeared. I returned to her lifeless body.

The young man had returned with the constable. "I saw him do it! I saw that nigger beat her to death after he had his way with her!"

I turned and walked away. I knew that another black man would hang. What made it even worse is that this man would hang for something he didn't do. I prayed to the Lord to take me.

"I am ready Lord. I cannot continue to watch helplessly as these people die for being black."

I stayed in the town for about a week. Unfortunately, I was right. After a quick trial, a young black man was hung for the crime of another. There was no justice in the world. I was well aware of the reason that I had died for these people's freedom. I hope that the North wins. I hope that this injustice will not continue.

It wasn't even a trial. It was a mockery of justice. I don't blame the court. I blame the liar that killed that girl and walked away without the truth ever being known. I walked away from the place I observed a second innocent black man die and I noticed, for the first time, the man responsible for the crime was in uniform. He was a Union soldier!

Again, I felt an empty feeling in my stomach. How could it be one of my own men? He walked away and I followed. As he mounted his horse, I took a good look at his face. I would see him again and I planned to be his judge, jury and executioner. I followed this soldier for a few days and he reported back to his unit.

Death came for him in battle. I observed the bullet rip through his face and he laid on the ground, gasping. I walked over to the spot where he lay.

"It seems that your sin has caught up with you. You have dishonored that uniform and the right to even be considered a man."

The young man stared up at me in terror. I knew he could see me and hear me as he approached death's door. I sat back and watched as it took four hours for death to finally claim him. When it did, he stood and looked at me. "How did you know?"

"I was there the night you raped and beat that girl to death. I watched you allow an innocent man hang for your crime. I pray that you be damned for your sins," I replied.

Before I could even finish that final sentence, a dark rider galloped toward us. He drew his sword and pierced the man through the chest. This man's soul was in torment and pain. I could see it. The dark horseman threw a rope around the man's neck and wrapped it around his saddle horn. The man's eyes widened and there was fire in them. The rider cracked a whip and dragged the man across the field, over the body that belonged to him, and disappeared into a black cloud.

I wasn't sure, but I think I witnessed that man being dragged to hell.

A few nights later, I was walking through a Union army encampment. The men were cleaning their guns and having a bite for dinner. There was a group of soldiers talking about what was going to happen in the morning. From what I could hear, two men were to be branded cowards. They had run from battle in the last skirmish and that was the army's way of making sure the shame would follow them for the rest of their days. It made me feel better to just be around the soldiers and remember the times I spent with my friends around the camp fire.

But, I was not too comfortable with the fact that two young men were going to have the letter "C" branded onto their faces for the rest of their lives I know that many men would have turned and run from their first skirmish as.

Morning broke and the captain had the two men tied to big wooden poles in the middle of the camp. The fire blazed and the branding irons were red hot in it. The captain stood and watched as the charges were read and the sentence was carried out.

My God, they were just boys; not much older than 16, I thought. The first boy screamed in anguish and fainted when they branded him. The second boy wet his pants and cried. I could not believe the utter brutality of what I had witnessed.

Those boys did nothing more than let their fear get the better of them and they were branded for it. I had heard of the practice but I had never witnessed it until then. Many of the men watching got sick. Some turned away and wept. I knew all would face death before facing a torture such as this and that is exactly the point the army was driving home by this act. It was still barbaric and I never agreed with it.

I walked away with a heavy feeling, in what was left of my very being, for those boys. This was not an act I would stand and witness again.

I walked for what seemed like a couple of days and ended up on a battlefield that reminded me of the one where my life ended. The battle had been over for a few hours and the moaning and groaning had nearly stopped. I came upon a Rebel soldier holding his younger brother in his arms. The boy was dying. He had a gunshot wound to his stomach and the older brother cradled him.

I watched as the younger brother gasped with his last breath, "John . . . John . . . there is an angel standing here." The boy stared directly at me and died with a little smile on his face. The older brother held the boy and cried.

That's when I wondered if this war was really worth fighting. I had seen more brutal acts after my own death than I had witnessed in battle. These Rebs were no different from us. I did not agree with slavery at all, but it may not have been a reason for boys to kill each other on the field of battle either.

I walked away and kept my direction toward the capitol. I only wished I could tell the President of the acts I had witnessed since my death. I was certain he would be as sickened as I was.

I walked on through the night and the next day, I met the young man that had died in his brother's arms.

"I have been following you, angel. I want you to show me the way to heaven."

"I am no angel. I am also a soldier that died in battle. I witnessed you die and I am sorry that you did. I cannot show you the way to heaven. I am not sure I will end up there," I responded.

The boy asked if he could walk with me for a while and I welcomed the company of another. We talked and I told him that even though we were on opposite sides, it no longer mattered because we now belonged to the afterlife.

We walked into the night and came upon a house. There was a black man standing outside and there were three men on horseback talking with him.

"We aren't far from my home. I recognize that black man by his face," the boy said. We approached and watched. The black man was saying to the three, "I am a free man. I have papers to prove that. You cannot search my house."

Two of the men jumped off of their horses. One pointed a rifle at the black man and the other entered the house. The black man turned to enter the house and the man with the rifle growled, "You move another muscle and I'll shoot you dead."

In a couple of minutes, the other man emerged with a woman and two small children. The man on horseback said, "You may be free, but them there are slaves. For harboring slaves, you die."

Without another word, the man with the rifle shot the black man in the face. The woman screamed and the boy that was with me ran to the fallen man's side.

"Why? Why did they shoot this man, angel?"

"I don't know. It is a senseless war."

The three men set his house on fire and rode off with the slaves. The boy knelt by the body for a long time. "I would never have fought for the South if I would have known."

I moved toward them and touched the boy's shoulder. "I would not have fought for either side. Both sides are guilty of many crimes that go unknown. The only people that know the truth can no longer tell anyone . . . people like you and me."

"I never knew his name, angel. I only knew him because he used to walk by my family's farm to sell his wares in town. He was a good man."

We sat there with the man until his house had smoldered to embers. "Angel . . . walk with me home. Walk with me to my family's farm."

I agreed and said a prayer for the fallen man before we turned to leave. I only wished that I had a physical body to be able to give this man a proper burial.

We walked for a few hours and finally reached the farm of my traveling partner. He asked me to wait for him outside while he looked in on his family. He was in the house for a while and a dog walked up to me and started sniffing around my feet. I looked at the dog he looked back at me, and walked away. That dog knew I was there; he could see me. I then realized that animals could still see me in some form.

The young man returned to the yard and told me he was going to stay around the farm and watch over his family. He said he knew the Lord would come for him after he watched over them for a while. I told him goodbye and I continued on my journey to the capitol.

I walked for what seemed to be days and I could see a camp in the distance. I headed in the direction of the camp and came upon another example of southern justice. Two men were beating up a young slave. They were kicking and hitting him in the chest and face.

I yelled at them to stop and remembered that they couldn't hear me. I tried to think of anything I could do to change the almost certain outcome. One of the men went to his horse and grabbed a rope hanging on his saddle. "Let's drag this bastard a while."

He tied the rope around the saddlehorn and made a loop to place on the young man's leg. I went over to the horse and screamed at it as loud as I could. The horse lunged forward and the rope tightened around the man's wrist before he could slip it onto the slave's leg. I clapped and yelled "Giddy up!" and that horse took off with that cruel bastard dragging behind screaming, "STOP, STOP!"

The other man jumped on his horse and took off in pursuit. I walked over to the young slave and whispered in his ear, "If you can hear me, you had better get up and run."

Somehow, that boy must have heard me. He scrambled to his feet and took off running the opposite way. I may have saved that boy's life that night. Maybe that horse heard me and maybe he didn't, but that young man was alive. I really hoped the horse would stop soon, but I did not regret making that horse run.

I tried to follow the young slave but I couldn't find him. I hoped that he would get away and make it to the North.

I continued on to the camp and listened to the southern soldiers play some fiddle music. Even though they were supposed to be my enemy, they were no threat to me. I stayed at the camp until they had all fallen asleep for the night.

I hoped it would not be much longer until I made it to the capitol. I walked on for a couple of days and, in a tree, I found my answer to where the young slave had gotten to. His lifeless body hung from that tree. I felt total anguish for that man. Fate had assisted me in helping his escape two nights earlier only to meet the business end of the noose encircling his neck. I prayed for that man's soul. I felt disgusted by the fact that a human life was considered worthless due to the color of skin.

If it were possible, I would have cut this man down and buried him properly. Once more, I had to leave someone in a very disrespectful way because I couldn't do anything to change it.

I knew that I had wandered for more than a year although, at times, it seemed like just a few days. I was determined to make it to the capitol and gaze upon one of the men I held most dear.

I continued my travels and witnessed many more things that sickened me. I could think of nothing better than seeing the president and just standing in the same room, even if he couldn't see or hear me.

I finally made it to Washington one night. I got my wish as I came face to face with President Lincoln.

And it would be one of the saddest days of my existence.

I am not sure of the time or the date, but I was now in Washington D.C. I walked toward the White House. I was hoping to see the President and just sit in the same room with him for a while. It was nighttime now.

I walked up on a lot of commotion outside of a theater. There was a crowd of people gathered around the house across the street from the theater. I hadn't seen that many people gathered in one place so quiet. They talked to each other but not much higher than a whisper. They all seemed very sad. I turned around and there, standing just outside of the theater, was the man I had traveled so far to see.

President Lincoln walked toward the crowd as if he were looking for someone. He asked a number of questions to various people but nobody would answer him.

I walked up to him. "Mr. President." I said.

"Hello there, soldier. How are you tonight?"

"I am doing well sir. It is my honor to meet you."

"Nice to meet you, son." The Mrs. and I were seeing a play in the theater over there, I got an excruciating headache and I must have fallen asleep. I awoke to everyone gone from the theater and I walked out here. You seem to be the only one that will talk to me."

"Mr. President, I would be honored to have a talk with you."

The President nodded.

"Why don't you walk with me back to the White House? I seem to have lost my escorts and you, being a soldier, can protect me."

My reply was, "It will be my pleasure, Mr. President."

We strolled on toward the White House and I told the President of the many things I had seen and encountered on my journey here. I explained to him that I was honored to serve in the army for his cause, but I was very apprehensive about the war.

"Well son, there are times that decisions we have to make are the hardest ones in our lives, but we do the best we can and that is all anyone can ask."

We had finally made it to the White House and I walked the President to the door. "Thank You for seeing me home, soldier. The guards will be relieved to see me home unharmed due to your kindness."

"The honor was mine, Mr. President, I only wish that you would have had more time to see things through."

Puzzled, the President looked at me and then he smiled and answered, "Well, son, re-elections can be won if we work hard enough at it."

I smiled. "Goodnight sir and God be with you and yours."

"Take care of yourself, son. Good night."

I walked away with a great feeling of pain in my soul. I knew that the President did not realize that he had died that night. I was not sure how it had happened but the fact that he could talk to me and see me showed me that it was true. I did not have any idea how to tell him so I decided not to. I hoped that he would find peace in his death and I prayed for his soul, and mine. "Lord, please look after President Lincoln and his family. May he find peace in his afterlife."

I had traveled for over a year to see that man but when I finally did, it saddened me to know that he was also a victim of a senseless war. I decided to return to the home where I grew up and to be thankful about having no more of this tragedy in my existence. I finally made it home and I recognized the smell of my mother's cooking immediately. I stayed around and watched my family. They would pray for me at dinner and I later found out, while my parents were talking, that the President had fallen victim to a gunshot to his head. "So much pain; useless suffering," I thought to myself.

One night, I was drawn through the kitchen and outside of the house. Everyone was asleep so I could not figure out what was going on.

I walked outside of the house and I heard a voice I had heard once before.

"Son, it is time to come home." There, before me, was President Lincoln.

"Mr. President, how did you find me?" "The Lord sent me for you. He said you would come with me if I asked so I am asking."

"What is it like, Mr. President? What is it like to be with the Lord?"

The President replied, "It is different for us all son, but your days of wandering are over. Someday your parents will join you there but, for now, we have much to talk about."

I walked across my parent's lawn with one of the greatest men that had ever lived. I had made sure that he had made it home the night of his death and he had now come to return the gesture

THE END

The Asylum

Written by: Sandra Wells

Chapter One

Arrival

I remember the day my mom brought me to this place in the spring of 1895. Just looking at it as we came up over the hill scared me. I asked my mom why we were going to such a place. She did not respond. As our carriage arrived at the front of the building, two men in what looked like uniforms of some kind were waiting outside. As my mom stopped the carriage, they reached in and grabbed me, pulling me out.

"Why are you doing this to me?" I screamed. "Help me! Help me, Mommy!" After they dragged me up the stairs toward the front door, I managed to twist myself to be able to see my mom driving away. "What have I done?" I yelled. "Mommy! Mommy!"

The men pushed me through the front doors and into a chair. They strapped my wrists and ankles down so I could not move. One of the men called to a woman named Miss Dottie. A harsh-looking woman in a long, black dress appeared from an office to my right and asked the men, "Who is this boy? Just another mouth to feed?" she asked, sarcastically.

They told her that my mom had messaged ahead and said I was out of control. My mother told them that I was hearing voices and acting as if the devil himself was in me so she brought me here to be shed of such an evil child.

I began to cry and tell them that my mother was lying. "I was not doing those things," I said.
"Shut up, you little whelp," she snapped at me. "I guess you better get used to being here with us. Do you have a name, young man? Answer me," she shrieked.

"Yes ma'am. My name is Josiah."

"Well, Josiah, there are certain rules you will be required to follow." As she listed the rules, I kept looking toward the front door, waiting for my mom to return. She must be playing a trick on me, I thought.

When she finished telling me the rules, I asked her, "Why am I here?"

She told me that my mom did not want me anymore so now I belonged to them. When I asked what this place is called, she told me "The Asylum."

Everything about this woman scared me. Her eyes were black as coal, I had never seen eyes that color before, and her face seemed to be full of anger. As she turned to walk away, she told the men to take me to my room in the children's ward and to make me comfortable. As they walked me down the long hallway, I could see men and woman wandering everywhere. Some were silently sitting on the benches that lined the hallway but some were moaning, or screaming profanity at each other, while others were violent against themselves and their surroundings. I asked one who the people are.

"That will be you when we get done with you, little man," one of the men responded with a look of disdain. When I started to cry, he snapped, "Shut up before I give you a reason to cry."

Suddenly, a man appeared in front of us, looking me in the eye and cooing, "Nice little boy. We will become good friends." Although I was unsure why, his words made my skin crawl.

"Jack, you get the hell out of our way," said the man to my left. Jack turned and skulked away.

Finally, after walking for what seemed forever, we arrived at the room that was to be mine. I looked through the double doors and saw children everywhere. If I had not seen them, I would have never known they were there. The silence was deafening but I could feel their pain and sorrow as if each one was stabbing my heart with a dagger. As we entered the area where I would be sleeping, the men threw me onto a makeshift bed. The mattress was so thin I could feel the wooden slats on my back.

"I will be good. Please don't hurt me," I whimpered. The men looked at each other and laughed. The one that spoke earlier looked at the other saying, "So, Sam, what do you think we should do to this one for talking to us?"

"I have an idea, Bill. Let's see how he likes going without anything to eat for a couple days."

"Good idea," the other said. They grabbed me again and strapped my wrists and ankles together like I was an animal. I begged them to let me go and the man named Sam shoved a rag into my mouth so I could no longer speak.

Because the men were so much bigger and stronger, there was no point in struggling. I started thinking about my mother. All I ever did was love her. I always did well in school and behaved myself. Why would she put me in such a place and abandon me?

As I watched the shadows grow longer through the window next to my bed, I dreaded the darkness that would soon come. I flipped and turned so I could see into the large room. I saw a boy younger than me come into my view. He was so thin and drawn and I wondered if I would end up like him. I suppose he saw me lying there so he came to the doorway and stared at me. His face was emotionless as if he did not see me at all. After a moment, he turned and walked away.

I had never gone without food before and my stomach hurt. I begged everyone I saw that night to help me as best I could since the rag was still in my mouth, but none of the children would help me. Suddenly, the same boy as before came into the room and walked over to my bed. He looked down at me and reached forward to pull the rag from my mouth. He told me to be quiet so the men would not return. I asked if he would free my straps so I could move.

"No, I can't do that," he said. "They would kill me if I did such a thing."

"What is your name?" I asked.

He told me he thought his name was Charlie, or at least that is what they called him; he was not sure anymore. I asked him why he was here and he said he did not know.

"What is this place?" I asked. Charlie told me it was a place where bad people get put and never get to go home anymore.

The first night was long but, as I watched the sun begin to stream through the window, I thought that maybe someone would return to bring me something to eat. As I lay there waiting, I watched the other children begin to roam the other room. I wondered if I had been forgotten. Then I saw Charlie enter the room with a piece of bread clutched to his chest.

"Here, I saved this for you," he said as he approached my bed. I thanked him and he left the room. In what seemed like many hours later, a woman entered the room. She was tall and thin, wearing a long, grey dress covered by a white apron I supposed she was a nurse. She did not smile, appearing cold when she spoke, and asked if I was going to behave myself. I nodded and she took the straps from my wrists and ankles. I did not say a word to her; I was too afraid. I suppose this is my life now so I better make the best of it. Little did I know that the night before, and the torment I had endured, was only the beginning of what would be revealed to me.

As I sat in the big room watching the activity, I saw Sam enter. He was there to take away a young girl who could not have been more than 5 or 6 years old. When he grabbed her by the arm, she suddenly became violent, screaming and thrashing about trying to get away from him. As he pulled her toward the main doorway, he turned and slugged her in the head making her fall to the floor. Undeterred, he grabbed her ankle and pulled her out the door.

The children in the room had scattered like roaches when a light is turned on. I wanted to help her but I knew I would end up back in my room strapped down again, or worse, so I sat quietly looking out the window. I could see nothing that looked familiar to me and I became very sad.

With nothing to occupy my time, the day passed slowly. I remained sitting by the window as Charlie walked up beside me. He turned to look around the room. I imagined he wanted to make sure none of the people who worked there was close enough to hear us talking because it was strictly forbidden.

He told me that this place was called The Asylum and it was run by Miss Dottie. He told me she is a mean lady that allows children to be hurt by the adults. He also said that no one who worked there would be nice to me.

"They don't love us. They do not care if they kill you. For them," he said,

"it is just one less mouth to feed."

I asked him why Sam would drag that little girl away like that.

"I don't know but when he brings her back, you watch, she will be bloody," Charlie said.

"How horrible!" I gasped.

"Make no mistake; it happens to all of us." He also asked if I had met Jack. When I nodded, he warned me to stay away from him if possible. "I have seen him sneak in here at night, take one of the children and they never come back. I have been lucky so far," he said and walked away.

As I watched Charlie walk away I wondered how he ever ended up here. He seemed normal enough to me. I figured it must have been the same way I got there. I wish I could remember all the rules; not knowing could mean my life. Just the thought scared me.

A few hours had passed when Sam returned with the little girl but this time she was in a wheelchair. Charlie was right. All down the front of her patient gown was blood. What had they done to this poor little girl, I wondered. It made me so mad to see her hurt like that but I knew what would happen if I tried to help her.

I wondered where in the world these men and women came from that worked there. Was this the hell that I had heard about in church, but for the living? It had to be; why else would such evil be taking place? I also thought about Miss Dottie and why she would be so hateful and run a place that would allow the torture of children. Who is this woman? Maybe someday I would find out more about her. I just knew that I did not want to have anything to do with her.

Suddenly, I heard a faint squeaking noise coming from the hallway. As I watched through the windows, I could see a nurse right outside the door. It was the end of the day and she pushed a cart with a big pot on it into the room. All the children grabbed a bowl from under the cart and she filled it with what looked like mush. I hated mush but I was too hungry to mind, so I got my share and sat down to eat it. After I ate the paltry amount I was given, I went to my bed and lay down for the night.

Chapter Two

The Days Become Weeks

Every day was the same in this place: the smells, the lack of food children being dragged from the ward returning with blank stares. Some returned covered in bloody clothes from the wounds all over their bodies. I felt lucky this had not been me as yet. Charlie and I talked when we could so as not to be noticed by anyone. For extra food or a day without treatments, the children told on each other for breaking the rules. The treatments, so called by the staff, were beyond torture I had heard. I did not know why they had not given me treatments as yet, but I had a feeling that would not last forever.

Time seemed to pass quickly but one day ran into the next as if there was no separation between them. Charlie and I became good friends. I became friends with many of the children in the ward but Charlie and I seemed to be connected, almost like we were brothers or something. We talked and laughed when no one was looking. It almost made being in the asylum bearable.

One night as I slept, I was startled awake by a strange noise. It almost sounded like the main doors to the ward swinging back and forth so I fell back to sleep without thinking much about it. The next day, when I came out into the large room, I did not see Charlie sitting in his usual spot. Quietly, I walked over to an older girl sitting by the door. I asked her if she had seen Charlie leave. She told me she had heard that Jack had paid a visit to our ward so she would not be surprised if that is where he was. She said she had a feeling he never would come back.

"No. No. I hope you're wrong," i said. I knew I dare not ask any of the people that worked there because they would beat me for breaking the rules. I sat by the window where I always did, waiting hours for Charlie to return. I put my head in my hands and began to weep silently. He was the only friend I had there. What would I do without him? The girl had been right; Charlie never came back to the ward.

Many times, as I sat looking out the window, I saw cars coming and going. I saw many police cars and wondered why they would allow the things that were going on here to happen. Don't they know or do they just not care?

A few days had passed since Charlie disappeared. That night, I dreamed that Charlie came to me. He told me that he had to go, but for me not to be sad because he was finally free. I begged him not to leave. As he walked away, I ran after him in my dream but he vanished, leaving me to face this place alone. The dream was so real; I woke up in a cold sweat looking around the dark room hoping to see Charlie. I finally realized it was only a dream and that I had lost my only friend forever. As I sat there on my bed, I wondered who Jack was and why they would allow him to come into our ward and take children like that. From what I had heard, he was a vile man that did unspeakable things to children, but no one ever told me what happened to the children other than they never came back. I did everything to try and not think of what must have happened to Charlie. I really missed having someone to talk to.

Days passed into weeks and weeks into months. Finally after several months had gone by, those who ran the asylum decided it was my turn for treatments. As I sat in my usual spot, I turned to see Bill standing there grinning down at me.

"Get up boy," he growled. "Are you going to come quietly or do I have to drag you to treatment?"

I told him I would come quietly, but he grabbed my arm anyway and walked me down the hall to a room full of instruments and strange devices. He told me to get onto the table and that if I screamed it would only be worse for me. Then a man I had never seen before entered the room. I think he was a doctor but I can't be sure.

Suddenly, he was using some of those instruments on me, slicing into my body. He told me that it would help clear my mind of the demons that tormented me. "Demons? What are demons?"

I wondered. I remember the pain was so intense and then I woke up and was covered in blood. I don't remember what happened but I hurt from whatever they did to me. How it happened did not matter at all. For weeks, the treatments continued. I gave up hope that I would ever get out of this place.

One day, a new girl arrived on the ward. She was an older girl, probably around the age of 15, named Lilah. She seemed like a normal girl, not like most of the children in this place. I heard that she was left there by her parents because they did not want her anymore. I waited for things to settle down and I walked over to her. She looked so sad and scared. I told her quietly how sorry I was to see her there. She just looked up at me and shook her head. I told her to be careful of breaking the rules, like Charlie had told me when I first arrived.

"Who were those two men that brought me in here? They scared me," she said. "They said they would have a good use for me because I was a tasty tart. Do you know what that means, Josiah?"

That did not sound good at all. They wanted to hurt her like so many before and I told her to be careful. "Stay out of sight when they come around and maybe they will forget," I urged. I knew that was not the case, but I did not want to scare Lilah more than she already was.

Night was the scariest time for me. I heard children's voices laughing. I would get up to look but found no one. There were also the sounds of people walking across the floor with no one in sight.

One particular night, the silence was broken by the blood curdling screams of a girl. It scared me so badly that I covered my head with the blanket and pillow but it did not silence the terrifying sound. It seemed to echo through the halls and my room for hours. Why is no one finding out who was screaming?

The next morning, I saw Lilah lying on her bed. Her gown was bloody and she had been beaten black and blue. She begged me to help her. I called for help but no one came. I asked what happened. She told me that Sam and Bill had come to get her in the middle of the night.

"They took me into a dark room down the hall where they pushed me to the floor and made me do unspeakable things with them both," she sobbed through swollen and cut lips. When she tried to fight them, they beat her. Even when her eyes filled with fear, she said, "I am not going to stay here, Josiah. I will not allow them to take me like that whenever they feel like it."

I asked her to take me with her. She looked me in the eyes and told me I couldn't go where she was going. I tried to get her to explain but she would not speak another word. I thought maybe it was best that I just give up the conversation. As she began to drift off to sleep, I sat beside her on the bed, stroking her hair. I felt so bad for her. I wish I could make her pain go away.

The next day when they came to wake us, I saw the doctor enter Lilah's room and quickly come back out, shaking his head and muttering about the stupid girl. I managed to find a place in the large room where I could see into Lilah's room. My mouth dropped open in shock to see her hanging from the ceiling rafter. I can honestly say that she had the courage to do something I had thought about many times. I was actually jealous because now both of my friends were free from this nightmare and I was still here.

Before I realized it, a year had passed since I arrived at The Asylum. Every day was the same; nothing ever changed other than watching the other children come and go. Many left almost as soon as they arrived. I barely would get to know someone and they would be gone, not only because of the treatments but from whatever else was being done to them. It did not matter to those that ran the asylum because one would die, two would take his place, and the cycle continued.

The ward suddenly began to fill with children. They slept on the floor, under beds, two or more to a bed and in chairs. Could Miss Dottie not find more suitable place for these children to sleep? We were like cattle to her and a way for her to make her almighty dollar.

Each day started the same with Sam and Bill entering the ward screaming at the top of their lungs, "Wake up you maggots" and "Get your asses up now." Then the blast of a siren would fill the entire ward and echo around the room. I am sure it was their way of torture for us all. I hated this place and each day only confirmed that to me. I wanted to leave, whether to go home to be with my mother or just to run as far away from this place as I could. But those thoughts would leave when I would look around at all the children, especially the really little ones.

A little girl had come to the asylum about a week before. She could not have been more than 4 years old. She sat silently, never looking at anyone, and she often cried for no apparent reason. Many times I would sit by her and ask what was wrong. She told me her daddy killed her mommy. He stabbed her to death and the police brought her here. Sarah was her name and she ended up here because she had no one to love her, just like me.

At night I took Sarah into my room and made a pallet on the floor beside my bed. I had to protect this poor little girl. I told her that I would be her big brother, take care of her and no one would hurt her as long as I was around. And I meant it, too. After the deaths of Charlie and Lilah, I told myself that I would do everything I could to protect these children from Sam and Bill. I even learned to sleep lightly to watch for Jack. I would never allow anyone to leave this ward with that man again.

One day, I got up to go to the bathroom early in the morning before anyone else had stirred. I stood in my doorway looking around. I don't believe that there was any space on the floor where children were not lying. As I made my way through the sea of sleeping bodies, I wondered where they all were coming from and why there were so many. Had there been some type of tragedy in the world where all these orphans had come from? Were they all sick like my mother had claimed I was?

Sarah and I were never apart; she followed me everywhere I went. I did not mind. Being 11 years old, I felt I had an obligation to watch over her. She was not like many of the other children. Most were very strange, many could not speak, but a lot of them were like me and Sarah. Most were abandoned children without a place to go and no one in the world to love them. I tried not to think about it because it made me too sad.

Months passed as I watched over Sarah, seeing that she got enough to eat. Sometimes I would go a couple days at a time without so much as a crumb of bread. The food they fed us was disgusting, often full of maggots. But I decided if one is hungry, any food is better than none.

One day after the meal cart came into the room, a young boy named Tommy, who was about 7, ran up to the nurse and tugged at her skirt, begging her to help him. She pulled away from him and walked quickly over to the pull rope on the wall attached to the siren. The noise from it scared us all because we knew what was about to happen to Tommy. He had just come to the ward a few days before and I guess he did not know the rules yet.

Before we knew it, Sam and Bill burst through the doors of the ward. Bill grabbed Tommy's arm, twisting it behind his back, and pushed him to the floor. I could not watch the abuse but I promised myself I would watch over the young ones. I took a deep breath and I ran toward Sam and jumped on his back, holding on tight. It was enough to distract Bill and he and released Tommy and pulled at me to get me to release my grasp on Sam's face.

"Let go of him you little heathen," Bill snarled. Then he started to beat on my back with a club and I fell hard to the floor. Tommy had scurried away in the confusion and stood watching in tears as they kicked and hit me until I could no longer move. Suddenly, Miss Dottie came into the room telling them to stop. She said that the state people and police had started asking questions. Rumors had reached the police of abuse and some of the adult patients and families filed reports.

She ordered them to put me to bed. After they threw me on my bed, I could hear Sarah crying beside me. "Don't cry, Sarah. I will be OK," I reassured her. So she lay down beside me on the bed and did not move from my side for the rest of the night.

Chapter Three

Secrets of the Asylum

The next morning, I woke with my body aching from the beating I received from Sam and Bill. I looked up and saw Sarah standing next to my bed staring down at me.

"How are you doing?" she asked softly.

I told her I was fine, even though every part of me hurt. She told me that she had heard some of the children talking about how maybe because of what Miss Dottie had said the night before, people might come to save us. I told her not to expect anyone like that; no one cared about us. I was bitter about being here but who could really blame me? I knew that nothing would change. The beating I got would not be the end of what was yet to come for me. Sam and Bill were cruel and because I had attacked Sam, it was far from over. I was terrified as to what my fate would be. I knew that somehow they would get back at me.

A few weeks went by with no retaliation for my actions and I grew more afraid with each day that passed. I knew that it would only be a matter of time. One evening after lights out, I sat on the edge of my bed pondering what I could do to get me and Sarah out of the asylum. I knew if we stayed much longer, something bad would happen to either of us. They had not yet started treatments on her and I knew it would not be too much longer. My worst nightmare was what if I could not protect her from Jack. It had been some time since his last visit to the children's ward. I could not stand the thought of losing Sarah to such a vile man.

Sitting on my bed, I could see out the windows of the main doors to the ward. It was dark in the hallway and I could not see anyone roaming past like during the day. I looked down at Sarah as she slept and hoped she was having nice dreams. At that moment, I realized that if I ever planned on getting out, I would have to get outside of this ward to find an escape. I had not left that ward since arriving at the asylum and I was scared but I knew it was the only way.

I moved silently to the doors and stood on tip toe to peek out the window to see if anyone was around. I saw no one; the hallway was empty with very few lights on. I pushed open one of the doors. It creaked, startling me and I whimpered. Once in the hall, I could see lights at the other end. As I quietly padded down the hall, I looked over my shoulder several times but saw no one.

I had never before noticed the putrid smell in the hallway. It smelled of urine and puke. The odor gagged me but I kept going. I knew I might not get this chance again. As I passed by the other wards, I peeked in to see if anyone was awake or wandering around. Still, I saw no one. Suddenly, I heard a man talking so I slipped into a dark doorway and waited. No one went by so I crept around the corner to see where the voice was coming from but saw no one.

Finally, I reached the lighted doorway. I did not see anything inside the room, not even a single stick of furniture. In one corner, I saw a metal cabinet with glass doors. It was full of bottles. The room had a strange odor I did not recognize. As I looked around the back side of the door, I saw another door. I went into the room and glanced at a brown bottle in the cabinet. It had a strange word on it. I could not read very well but it was spelled E-T-H-E-R. I wondered what it was used for. When I opened the bottle to smell the contents, I felt really dizzy. I put the bottle back and thought I better get back to exploring when I heard footsteps. I went back to the door into the hallway and still saw no one. I was sure I had heard footsteps but I needed to find out where that door led to. I went back in to the room and opened the door slowly.

The room was dark and smelled horrible. What was that smell? I found a lantern and lit it. I couldn't believe my eyes! Stacked against every wall in the room were bodies of men and women. There was blood everywhere. I vomited as I ran from the room. I did not even take the time to shut the door or put out the light. I just ran back to the ward. By the time I reached my bed, I was shaking like a leaf. What had happened to these people? Why were they there?

Where was everyone? Had some maniac come in the night and killed everyone? I picked up Sarah and put her on my bed. How would I ever protect her from such a horrible fate? I sat the rest of the night waiting and watching every shadow. I was afraid to close my eyes. When the sun finally peeked through the window, I walked out into the ward. No one was awake yet so I peeked into the hallway. Still not seeing any movement, I went back to the room and waited for the morning wake-up call.

At least that had not changed; Sam and Bill came bursting through the door at 7 a.m. as always. To be honest, I was actually glad to see them. As Sarah and I ate what little food we had, I saw Miss Dottie walk by the doors as she usually did in the mornings. This time, however, she seemed in a hurry as if she was late for something. I told Sarah to stay put and I walked over to the ward doors to look out. I could see and hear her screaming at the staff. I could not hear everything that was being said but I heard a lot.

She was frantic. She said that state people were coming to inspect the asylum and that it was time to get rid of . . . but I could not hear what she said after that. She also mentioned a lady that would soon be there to look at the children and their living conditions. The woman's name was Angeline Taylor," some goody two shoes who was going to ruin everything that they had built there if something was not done soon, she said. As I strained to listen, Sarah came up beside me and asked what I was doing. I told her not to worry and we turned and walked back to our usual spot in the room and sat down to play a game.

The day passed slowly and I knew that, once everyone was asleep, I would have to make another trip. Something very strange was going on and I wanted to know what it was. Plus, I had to find a way out for Sarah and me. After the lights went out, I lay on my bed wondering what had upset Miss Dottie so much. I often wondered where she came from and how she could be so cold-hearted.

When everyone was finally asleep, I crept into the hallway. Again, the hallway was silent and dark and I walked slowly, but this time in the opposite direction. As before, each ward was dark and lifeless—or so I thought. As I came to one of the wards, I looked through one of the windows to see Sam and Bill going from patient to patient, putting the white coats on to restrain them. As I watched, I heard someone walk up behind me. Afraid to turn, I slowly glanced over my shoulder to see Sarah standing there.

"What are you doing, Josiah? How come you are out here?"

"Shhhh! Do you want those mean men to come and kill us?" I whispered.

She shook her head, eyes wide with fear.

I managed to get Sarah back into bed and asleep before I struck out again. I walked back to the room where I had seen Sam and Bill and found them gone, but the patients were still strapped in coats and restraints. I felt bad for them but knew I could do nothing to help them. I continued my journey down the hall. As I reached the end, I heard a dragging noise and muffled voices crying for help. As I turned the corner, I saw Sam, Bill and two other men dragging people into the center of the large room. Once there, they smashed their heads over and over with a big hammer and a metal bar of some kind. I must have gasped because Sam turned to see me watching them. That's the last thing I remember.

The next thing I remember is being back in my room, watching Sarah sleep. I thought that was odd but I figured Sam must have knocked me out and brought me back here. As I watched the sun come up and heard the usual morning routine begin, Sarah sat up on her bed and looked around as if she was missing something.

"Sarah, what are you looking for?" I asked. She did not answer me.

"Sarah, are you alright? What is wrong with you?" I asked. She got up and walked into the ward as if she did not even see me. As I watched her wander around the ward, I got worried. She would stop and talk to some of the other children, asking something I could not hear. Finally, I caught up to her; she was frantic.

"Where is Josiah? Why did he leave me?" she asked Tommy. He told her he had not seen me this morning. I did not understand. What was wrong with them? I am right here. Couldn't they see me? I kept screaming, "I am right here! Sarah! Sarah!"

I walked away thinking they must all be crazy and sat down in my usual spot by the window. I glanced up and there, standing in front of me, was Charlie.

"But . . . but . . . but . . . you're dead," I stammered.

"So are you, Josiah," he replied with a smile.

"No. I can't be dead. How can I still be here if I am dead?" I asked.

He told me that Sam had killed me. He said Sam hit me in the head until I was dead.

"No. No. No," I said frantically. "How am I going to take care of Sarah and protect her? I can't leave her. I promised."

Charlie told me that, for some reason, he had been here since Jack killed him. "You can still take care of Sarah. I have been watching over you both for a long time, Josiah," he told me.

"So what happens now?" I asked Charlie. He told me I could stay if I wanted to; it was my choice. He decided it was time for him to go. He told me that now it was up to me to take care of myself and Sarah.

"Watch her closely, Josiah. He will be coming for her soon." And with that, Charlie was gone. Sarah was sobbing with no one there to comfort her. I was so sad. It's my entire fault this happened. Oh God, please let me watch over my friend, I prayed. I felt so strange; my head was spinning. How could I let Sarah know that I was still here with her?

In what seemed like a blink of an eye, a week or two had passed. Sarah was not herself anymore. All she did was stare out the window. I believe she thought I had left her by leaving the asylum.

"Why can't you hear me, Sarah? I am right here beside you," I told her. I reached out and touched her hand and she looked up as if she felt my hand on hers. She smiled a little, which made me feel better. At least I knew that she was not completely gone.

This place had a way of doing that to people no matter who they were. I don't know how much time had passed but one night, as I sat in the corner watching Sarah sleep, I heard footsteps and looked up to see Jack come into the room.

"You bastard," I said. "You have come for the wrong little girl." Anger welled up inside me and I struck the door. I pushed it so hard it slammed with a loud bang. The noise startled everyone in the big room. I guess it even scared Jack because he ran from the room like he was being chased. You have no idea how good it made me feel to know that I saved Sarah from a fate worse than death, as I now understood.

Over the next few weeks, I watched Sarah become more withdrawn. She would not talk to anyone. Tommy tried on several occasions to get her to play a game but she refused. I knew the only way I could save her was find out more about what was going on here at the asylum. I needed to try to tell the state people what was happening.

Chapter Four

Changes

When Sam and Bill entered the ward that morning, something was different. There was no screaming at the children, no siren. They just walked around to each child waking them with a nudge before leaving the room. Next entered the nurse with two carts full of regular breakfast items like bacon, eggs and toast . . . food none of the children had seen since being here. The children all lined up as usual and got their plates full of food all except Sarah who sat by the window. I just shook my head and watched the nurse, who had always been so mean to us all, walk over to Sarah to hand her a plate full of food.

Sarah glanced up but went back to staring out the window. The nurse set the plate down and walked away. What was going on? This must be a dream. I walked over to the door and saw a bunch of men and a nice looking woman standing in the hallway making notes and looking around. Miss Dottie was standing there with her head down as if she was a child being scolded. I laughed to see her so upset. These must be the state people we had heard about. Finally they had come to see the horrors of the asylum. Maybe they could end the patients' nightmare.

I was excited, even though it was too late for me. I watched, staying close to Sarah as the state people entered the ward with Miss Dottie. I wished I could talk to these people. As they stood by the front doors, they looked around, making notes, shaking their heads and quietly speaking to Miss Dottie. The woman I spoke of earlier was a nice looking woman, dressed as if she was a nurse. She walked around the room talking with the children. One of the younger boys approached her and tugged on her skirt. She looked down at him with a pleasant, caring smile and she reached out to stroke his hair. She seemed to truly care about him. As she made her way around the room, she noticed Sarah sitting alone by the window and approached her slowly.

"Hello. What is your name, my dear?" she asked Sarah. "My name is Angeline. Will you speak with me?" Sarah turned to look at the woman and her eyes filled with tears.

"My name is Sarah. Are you here to help me find my friend?" she asked.

A strange look crossed Angeline's face and she asked Sarah who she was talking about.

"My friend Josiah," Sarah said, tears running down her cheeks. "I don't know what happened to him. He loved and took care of me and now he is gone."

"Don't worry, Sarah. I will find out what happened to him," Angeline reassured her. Sarah stood up and wrapped her arms around Angeline's waist. She hugged her so hard, I did not think she would ever let go.

"My dear, sweet little girl. I am going to help you and all the children. That is why I am here." One of the men called to Angeline, telling her it was time to move along. Sarah finally backed away and the woman told her that she would see her again very soon.

The state people disappeared through the doors and Sarah actually waved and smiled at Angeline. I was thrilled that Sarah had someone to watch over her again. Just as I thought that everything would be fine, in walked Sam and Bill. They glared at the children the way they usually did and told them that if one of them ever told what had been happening here they would never see the light of day again.

"You little bastards will regret opening your mouths, so I suggest you keep them shut," Sam said.

Bill told them this changes nothing and they turned and walked out of the ward. At least while the state people were there, Sarah would be safe so I decided to follow Sam and Bill to see if I could find out anything new. I was determined to figure out a way to see them go to prison forever for what they and Miss Dottie had done. I also wanted to find out where Jack was. I especially wanted to keep an eye on him.

I followed the pair down the hallway and looked into one of the other wards, seeing much of the staff standing around talking. I decided to listen in since no one could see or hear me. One of the nurses was saying that she had enough of this place, and something about not going to prison for anyone. She also said she was going to get the hell out of here before she came up missing, too.

Some of the pieces started to make sense about the mysterious disappearance of so many patients. Of course, I already knew some of the goings on but there was more to it. The only way I could make sure that Sarah and the other children stayed safe was finding out the whole story about the asylum, Miss Dottie and the other staff. After listening for a few more minutes, I thought I should get back to following Sam and Bill. I had the feeling they were the main source of the clues I needed. My biggest problem was how I would ever let anyone know what I learned. They could not see or hear me. I was sure there had to be a way.

As I stood in the hallway, I watched the state people leave through the front doors. A sudden feeling of dread came over me because I knew things were about to get really bad really fast. I walked down the hall to where Miss Dottie was standing and I saw Sam and Bill come out of her office. If nothing else, I had to hear what they were talking about.

"Sam, where did you put Jack?" Miss Dottie asked.

"I chained him up down in the basement in THE room," Sam responded.

"Go get rid of him. I don't care how, just do it," Miss Dottie hissed.

Sam nodded and walked away. I had to find this place they were talking about. Maybe I could get a clue as to what happened to some of the children that came up missing. I already knew a lot about where the adults had gone, even though I did not know how they disposed of all those bodies.

I followed Sam into the basement. He headed down a long passageway to a secluded area where I saw piles of brick everywhere. The wall on one side of the room looked new. As he stepped behind this wall, he lit a couple torches that were there. When the torches lit the room, I could see the large room was piled with children's clothing, shoes and girls' hair ribbons. I saw a couple of mattresses on the floor. Both were covered in what looked like blood. I did not want to think about why they were there and what had happened on them.

Walking forward to where Sam was standing, I could see another smaller room and there, chained to the wall, was Jack. He begged Sam to let him go.

"You have to be kidding me, you son of a bitch," Sam spat. With that, he raised a pistol and shot Jack in the head at point blank range. He must have shot him six times as I stood there and watched Sam do exactly what I had wanted to do for so long. That man had taken my best friend from me and I felt no remorse for thinking such horrid thoughts. He deserved what he got.

I wanted to get a closer look at the room where Jack now lay dead. As I walked around the corner, on the right side of the room, I saw a partially-built wall and something even more strange. A strand of blonde hair flowed over one of the bricks in the wall. I walked up to the wall and looked into a hole where I saw the hair. Inside was the skeleton of what must have been a girl. She was still dressed in what looked like a dress. The skeleton was small so it must have been a young girl. Next to her were two more skeletons, although I could not see much of them.

I backed away from the wall, wondering if this is where Jack brought his victims. Then it occurred to me that Charlie's body must be here, too. An overwhelming sadness came over me. I felt weak as I made my way back into the large room and sat down in a corner. Why would anyone be so cruel? How was I ever going to tell anyone about the horrors I had just witnessed. I looked up to see Sam un-cuff Jack's body from the wall and drag it to a corner of the room where he had dug a shallow grave and shove him into it.

"See you in hell, Jack," Sam snarled as he covered the body with dirt. "To hell with this," he muttered, "That old bitch can take care of her own messes from now on." He dropped the shovel he had been using and walked out of the room and back down the long hallway.

I got back up to the ward as quickly as I could to watch over Sarah. Something bad was about to happen and I was ready to do anything I could to keep her safe.

The next morning was as quiet as a grave with no movement in the hallways. I did not see the adult patients wandering around like they normally would be by now. As I walked back in to wait for everyone in the ward to get up for the day, I wondered if this nightmare would ever end for Sarah. I did not want to stay here anymore. It was time for me to go to heaven or wherever dead people went. I was finally free of my tortured existence but I could not leave until I knew Sarah had someone to love and care for her.

In what seemed like hours later, Angeline returned as she promised. It was too bad she could not see or hear me because I was screaming at the top of my lungs with joy. Of course by this time, the children were all up and roaming around the ward. Sarah, sitting in her place by the window, turned to see Angeline and ran to hug her. Angeline smiled down at Sarah. I got close enough to hear them speak and Angeline told Sarah she would soon be going to a new home. Apparently she had done some checking and found that Sarah had grandparents who had been looking for her after her mother was killed. The state was checking into the police department that had brought Sarah to the asylum because they never looked for her family. Sarah was speechless; she just clung to Angeline. I was so happy for her, even though I knew I would lose another friend. It was alright; she would be safe and sound.

As her attention moved to the rest of the children around her, Angeline told them all that soon they would be leaving this horrible place to go live in a newly-built orphanage where they would be taken care of properly. The children that could talk jumped around, screaming happily. Those who could not tried to smile. As I watched, I wondered why the state people had not come sooner. I would have had a chance to still live my life; now it is too late for me. Where would I go when this was all over? Would I go to heaven? I had much left to do, though. Even though Sarah would soon be gone, I had to make sure that Miss Dottie, Sam and Bill would pay for their crimes.

Chapter Five

The Asylum Ends

Days became much brighter in the ward. The children never had to see much of Sam or Bill anymore because Angeline stayed in the ward most of the time.

One day began as most did lately. Angeline made sure everyone was well fed, got proper baths and some attention. They all began to get some color back in their cheeks and thrive once again. Once a week, a state doctor came to check on the children's health progress. No treatments were allowed unless the state doctor approved them.

Sarah began to smile and laugh again thanks to Angeline. The day finally came when an older couple arrived and came into the ward. As they looked around at the children, their eyes fell on Sarah. Apparently, she was the spitting image of her mother as a child and they recognized her immediately. The woman's eyes welled with tears as she called out, "Sarah! Sarah!" When Sarah turned to look at them, Angeline looked up as well.

"Sarah, these are your grandparents. They are here to take you home now," Angeline reassured her.

Sarah ran into their arms, tears streaming down her pink cheeks. "Oh, Nana! Papa! Where have you been? I thought you did not love me anymore."

"My sweet baby, we have been looking for you since your mommy died. We could not find you until this nice lady sent word that she had found you," her grandfather said.

Suddenly, Sarah became serious and said, "Nana, Papa, I can't leave here yet. I don't know what happened to my friend, Josiah."

I was so surprised she had not forgotten me!

"Sarah, you need to go now, my dear," Angeline said softly. "I promised you that I would find out where he is and what happened to him. I will let you and your grandparents know when I find out. Is that alright?"

Sarah nodded sadly. Her grandparents asked who Josiah was. Sarah told them that he had watched over her and then, one night, he left and never came back.

"You mean he left the asylum?" Angeline asked.

"No," Sarah said, "He left this room and I have not seen him since."

"I will find out what happened to him, Sarah. I promise."

Giving Angeline one last hug, Sarah turned and walked out of the ward, hand-in-hand with her grandparents. I was glad she would be able to grow up normally.

As the weeks passed, the other children began to leave for their new home at the orphanage. Angeline worked hard to prepare the children both physically and mentally for their trip. I watched her often as she sat by the window where Sarah and I often sat. I wondered what must have been going through her mind. On the rare occasions when she left the ward, Sam and Bill wandered in. The children that remained got scared all over again. It was time for me to get back at them somehow. I felt that I had to scare them away for good.

One night, when Angeline was gone for the night, Sam entered the ward quietly. He walked over to one of the boys asleep in his bed and looked as if he was going to pick him up. I ran as fast as I could and shoved him. It did not have much effect, but he stopped what he was doing. I am not sure how I did it but I got his attention by kicking the metal leg of the bed. It made a loud clanking noise and he turned to look. Apparently, he could see me standing not more than two feet in front of him because his eyes got big as saucers and his mouth dropped open. His feet began to backpedal as he stumbled over toys, beds, chairs and whatever else was in his path as he tried to run from the room. I chuckled. That was too easy. From that point on, I managed to allow the staff to see me whenever I felt like it, giving them a jolt and letting them know I was watching. That was the most fun I had since I was brought to the asylum.

As you can imagine, there is not a whole lot a ghost has to do but wander around. One day, as I walked down the hall, I swear I saw Jack enter one of the adult wards. How was that possible? Is he a ghost stuck here, too? I hope not. If I can not figure out how to get out of here does that mean I am stuck with him for eternity chasing me around this building? I have to get out of here. As vile as he was in life, I can only imagine what he will be like in death. I did all I could to avoid him, but I knew one day our paths would cross.

The ward was down to about 20 children now and Angeline spent most of her time at her desk in the ward writing on charts for each child. One day, Bill came into the room. He seemed very different for some reason so I kept a close eye on him. He stumbled over to the desk. Angeline looked up and asked what he wanted.

"You are a beautiful woman and I just want to get to know you better," he slurred.

"Who do you think you are?" she asked him. "Do you honestly think the state does not know what has been going on here at the asylum?"

He snatched her up by the arms and said, "You have no idea what I am capable of bitch so I would watch my tongue if I were you." He dropped her back into her chair and staggered out of the room.

I felt bad for her. Her face was pale and she looked terrified for just a moment. But she quickly regained her composure and went back to work.

A few more days passed when I followed Miss Dottie into her office. Her office seemed more like a small apartment than an office. She had fine furniture and embellishments everywhere. She began to talk on the phone so I listened to see if I could determine what she was up to. I had no idea who she was talking to, but she seemed to be making plans for something. She told the other person that times are getting desperate.

"That nosy little bitch is ruining everything," Miss Dottie said into the phone. "She is asking too many questions about that kid named Josiah and I need to get rid of her before she finds out the truth. What should I do?"

Apparently, the person on the line must have told her what she needed to do because she quickly hung up and darted into the hallway to call for Sam and Bill. Miss Dottie ordered them to keep an eye on Angeline.

"Thomas says we need to fix it so she can't tell anyone what she has discovered so far," she said. Smiling, Sam and Bill looked at each other, and told her it would be their pleasure to take care of it. I could not let them hurt Angeline.

I ran as fast as I could back to the ward. I knew I would probably scare her but I had no choice. I had to tell her what I had just heard. But how was I going to do that?

She was sitting at the desk when I bumped it to get her attention. She felt the movement and looked up. I knew she saw me as the color drained from her face. I motioned to her to follow me. She had to know the truth.

"Who are you? Josiah, is . . . is . . . that you?" she stammered. I nodded and motioned again for her to follow me. She rose from the desk and moved toward me. I stayed ahead of her, but glanced over my shoulder to be sure she was following me. It was so hard to stay visible; I was losing energy quickly but I got her to the basement doorway and pointed at the door. She opened the door to reveal the steps leading down to the basement. I knew she could not see me anymore but, making noises, I stayed with her to lead her in the direction of the room where I had seen Sam kill Jack.

Finally, we reached the first large room where I had seen the children's clothing and the mattresses. I managed to move one of the torches on the wall so she would light it. When she saw the clothing, ribbons, shoes and bloody mattresses, she burst into tears. Then I made a noise from within the room where Jack died and was buried by Sam. She had removed the torch from the wall and was looking around when she saw the blonde hair. She slowly walked toward the opening in the wall and peeked inside. She gasped and stumbled backward in shock.

With tears streaming down her face, she screamed, "Who are these animals that they could do such a thing to these children?" She turned to leave the room just as Sam and Bill appeared out of the darkness.

"Hello," Bill said.

"What do you think you are doing down here, you bitch? I guess you know we can't let you leave," Sam growled. "I have wanted this tasty tart for months now." And he pushed her to the floor.

She screamed and screamed to no avail. They both attacked her repeatedly. All I could do was cry as I watched in horror. When both were finally spent, Angeline laid on the cold concrete weeping.

"Now that is over, we have no more use for you," Sam said. And he slammed a brick into her face over and over until she was dead and no longer recognizable. I cried because I thought I was alone again. Now who was I going to tell about the evil that I had lived with in the asylum? I squatted in the corner, blaming myself for what had just happened as I watched as Sam and Bill sealed her body in the wall like they had done to countless others. All is lost and no one will ever know, I thought with despair.

For what must have been weeks, I sat on my old bed in my room hoping for a miracle that someday, somehow, the truth would be known. Suddenly, I heard a noise and turned to see Angeline standing in the doorway.

"Hello, Josiah. So, we finally get to see and hear each other," Angeline said with a warm smile. I asked why she stayed and she told me she didn't want to leave me alone.

"We have a task, young man. We will not allow Miss Dottie, Sam or Bill to get away with all the pain and suffering they have put upon people here. It is their time to be punished. I will not leave you by yourself, Josiah. I will stay with you and we will leave together when the time is right."

I agreed and we sat on the bed talking about all that I had seen and experienced at the asylum. I told her how I got left there by my mother, how Charlie disappeared, why Lilah had hung herself and how I stayed after I was murdered by Sam. I told her about "treatments" and what a vile man Jack was. I told her everything. It had been so long since I had spoken to anyone that I guess I got a little carried away with myself.

She just sat there listening, almost as if in shock to hear of all the horrors we had all endured.

"Angeline, why are we still here?" I hoped she would be able to give me some answers but she admitted she didn't know. She insisted we would learn together.

The next day, Angeline and I were walking the halls, because there was nothing else to do, when we saw a bunch of men in uniform enter the front doors. I asked Angeline if she knew who they were.

"Those are the state police and I think they are here to arrest Miss Dottie and the others. They have been working for a long time on gathering enough evidence to arrest them," she said, and I could hear the excitement in her voice. "It is over, my little friend. They will never see the light of day again once they discover all of our bodies in the basement."

We moved closer to hear what was going on and I heard one of the policemen tell Miss Dottie, Sam and Bill, as they were being handcuffed, that their accomplice had been caught, too. Apparently, the chief of police and a number of other officers had been arrested after being caught red-handed with a small child that had been kidnapped. They had been bringing children there for years and making money by selling them to Miss Dottie. Some she kept, but many older children were turned out for prostitution and she got kickbacks. Then we found out that Miss Dottie had been a Madame who got caught. She made a deal with the police chief and opened this place as a front for their prostitution, sales of body parts and all kinds of evil things.

Finally, after arresting all the staff that remained, they put them in squad cars and drove away. A few of the policemen stayed to start the arduous task of collecting evidence. Angeline and I thought our task was complete, but they never found the bodies in the basement.

"I bet that is why we have not been able to leave, Angeline," I said and she agreed.

Once they thought they had everything, the police left the building. We watched as each door was bolted with heavy chains and the windows sealed to keep out intruders. The asylum was now closed. So, now what are we supposed to do?

Chapter Six

Trapped

Time passed as it always did. Angeline and I spent most of our days wandering the hall. Little did we know the complexity of the asylum and its hold on so many. Apparently, Angeline and I were not the only ones stuck in this place. The halls, now dark and dank, revealed many others that remained within its wall. Many of them were as they were in life, lost and confused from the tortures of their minds, and others wailed in torment of being stuck there with no release.

By now, several living people had broken into the asylum, writing on the walls, breaking doors and windows. Time took its toll and the building fell into disrepair. We had no idea how many years had passed, but we remained trapped. One day, Angeline and I made our way to the basement to look for more clues so we could eventually tell someone. As we happened to enter the area where she had been killed, we saw Jack coming from a small room to our left. He looked directly at us and laughed in a most evil way.

"Now that I know you are here, I will never allow you to leave the asylum," he said. We turned and nearly ran from the room to get away as quickly as possible.

"How are we ever going to get out of here now? Did you hear what he said? He is never going to let us leave," I whimpered, shaking from the encounter.

Angeline put her arm around me and reassured me. "Don't worry, Josiah. I don't believe that will be up to him. That is only up to God, not that evil so-and-so." I told Angeline that I was glad she had stayed with me.

As we sat next to the window one day, we turned to see Jack standing in the doorway to the ward. As he walked toward us, the chairs and bed frames left behind actually slid sideways to clear a path for him. Angeline stood in front of me to block his path, but to no avail. He grabbed me with such force I felt like I had been hit in the chest with a board. The three of us struggled as Angeline tried to protect me. He just laughed, saying he did not "get the chance to have you as mine in life but you both are now mine. None of us will ever leave this place, I swear."

Finally, we broke free and ran away as fast as we could.

"You can't get away from me . . . EVER," Jack bellowed.

From that day on, we spent our days just trying to avoid Jack. The building itself, now void of life, provided echoes and constant reminders of Jack's presence. We heard objects moving, doors slamming and his vile laugh. He was such a powerful force that none of us were a match for him.

I always thought of death as being a release. I already had endured hell in the asylum. After having several encounters with Jack, Angeline and I looked everyday for a new place to hide from him, even if for only a short time. One day, as we entered the room where I had found all of the adult patient bodies before I died, I told Angeline what I had seen. Neither of us were happy about being in this room, but it seemed the only place to find some peace. Since the bodies were long gone, we could see the walls were lined with tables where the bodies had been piled.

"I wondered what they did with everyone?" Angeline pondered.

"I don't know, but look over there," I replied, pointing. In one corner, behind a shelf, was an opening or doorway. I wondered if the state police had even been in this room. If we could see the opening, why wouldn't they?

As we entered the hidden room, we were struck speechless at the number of wooden shelves. On each shelf were several jars. Inside the jars were body parts. We saw eyes, hearts and organs of all types. Where did they come from?

Now, not only did we have to tell someone about the basement and its false walls but also about this. This must mean all those body parts came from the adult patients I saw that night and the ones I saw Sam and Bill bludgeon to death. How would we ever find a way to tell anyone about what we found?

Sickened, we could not stay in the room. Instead, we went to find another hiding place.

At the end of the hall, we found a door that had been pulled open. As we looked closely, we could see the outdoors.

"We can leave the building through here, Josiah," Angeline said excitedly.

I was scared to cross the threshold because that would mean I would be leaving the only home I had known for many years, but it was nice to know we could get away from Jack. As we walked forward to leave, we heard someone approaching behind us. We turned to see Jack so we rushed through the door to escape his grasp. As we looked, Jack was stopped by some invisible force. Something or someone was keeping him from leaving the building. Why could we leave and he was trapped? Angeline suggested it was because of all the evil he had done in his life. As we turned to get away, we noticed rows and rows of grave stones as far as the eye could see. Maybe because it was sanctified ground, evil could not enter it. As we roamed the graveyard, we found a place under a beautiful oak tree to rest. It was the best day I could remember in my whole time of being trapped within the asylum. We agreed to remain here until we saw a living person and then do our best to get their attention.

I am not sure how long we had sat there, but we watched the seasons pass many times. Buildings began to spring up around the asylum grounds; some were homes and others looked like larger buildings. We watched as the asylum fell into ruin. The patients that remained peeked out of windows and doors. We wondered why we were allowed to leave the building when the others had to remain within its confines. We saw Jack from time to time, staring at us, but still unable to leave. Oftentimes, we wandered the grounds to determine who was buried in the graveyard. The cement blocks, that we presumed were headstones, were marked only with a number or initials.

One day during our wanderings, we found one of the remaining buildings that had a large chimney attached to it. As we entered, we saw what looked like large ovens. Everywhere in the rooms of this building there were shoes and rotting clothing. Angeline told me that she had once seen a place like this. She said that sometimes when people die, they put them in these ovens to burn the bodies rather than bury them in the ground. A couple of the doors had broken away from the oven and inside we saw piles of bone and ash. Angeline believed this was all that remained of the bodies I had seen. As we moved around the rooms, we found rotting ledgers. They were filled with lists of names. We could not believe that many people had died in the asylum. Apparently the police had not come out to this building; otherwise, we were sure they would have gathered this evidence. We wondered why the police had been so careless.

The time had come when we decided to venture back into the asylum. Angeline and I knew that one day we would get an opportunity to tell someone about this place. We found a door that had been pulled away from its frame so we entered quietly. There was no Jack in sight so we found a quiet room and sat silently in the dark. Where were the other ghosts? Had they been able to hide this long without Jack finding them?

The next morning, he walked right by our hiding place. He did not notice us at first but the shock of seeing him again caused me to gasp. He turned and, with his evil laugh, chased us around the building as he had before. Although it was not the smartest idea to come back into the building, we knew the day would come when he would be sent straight to hell.

Chapter Seven

Finally Saved

Our existence continued with Jack controlling all who remained. He never allowed us close enough access to any exits again. One day, while looking out of the window in the front of the building, we saw one of those horseless carriages pull up. A man and woman got out. Standing by the machine, they scanned the building with their eyes. Suddenly, they walked toward the asylum with strange looking objects in their hands and hanging from their necks. They walked up the stairs to the front door and, using a key, unlocked it and entered the building. Were these people here to save us?

Suddenly, out of the corner of my eye, I saw Jack charging toward them. As I turned to look at the people, the woman said she could feel something bad here. Jack stopped abruptly, probably shocked that someone actually had the nerve to enter his domain. Then with a swift motion of his arm, he struck the man across the chest and he flew backwards about 4 feet into a wall. The woman ran over to him and asked if he was alright. He said he was and stood up.

He turned to the woman and said, "Katie, we are going to need help with this place. It is huge and now we know we have got to rid this building of whatever that was for sure."

"We can do that tonight if you want," she said. "I will gather the team and we will come back."

We watched them leave the building, knowing that finally we might have someone to tell about our discoveries . . . if we could find a way to talk to them. After the people left, we did not see Jack. We wondered if his contact with the living had affected him in some way, so we kept a wary eye for him to return. Angeline and I sat talking about how worried we were for these people. Jack had a strong hold on this place and all of its ghostly inhabitants. How could they make him leave?

Before we knew it, the shadows of evening crept through the broken windows. We sat in Miss Dottie's office waiting to see if the people would return. Just when we began to despair that they would not, we saw a number of driving machines pull up in front of the building. Looking out the window, I saw a woman outside staring as though she could see us.

"Hello! I can see you looking at me," she said. "My name is Desiree. I am here to help you." A man walked up beside her and asked what she saw. She told him that there was a woman and a boy of about 13 looking at them from those windows, pointing right at us. Angeline and I just looked at each other, mouths hanging open in disbelief that this woman could see us.

"Brad, I need to get inside and talk to them," she told him. "They need our help. I can feel it."

Once inside, we watched as they set down black cases. When they opened them, I could see a lot of strange devices. It scared me because the last time I saw strange things like that, Sam and Bill took me to treatment and they hurt me with them. I backed away. I had no reason to believe these people were here to harm us, but I was not about to take any chances.

While the others gathered several pieces of equipment, Desiree walked into the office. Both Angeline and I backed into the far corner of the room. She said, "Please do not be afraid of me or my friends. We are here to help you."

The woman we saw earlier in the day entered the room

"Where are they, Des?" Katie asked.

"They are over there in the corner and they are scared of us. Maybe you can explain what the device in your hand is used for so they understand."

"We will not hurt you. This device in my hand will allow us to hear your voice if you will speak with us," Katie said.

I giggled. How could they ever be able to hear our voices when we are dead? Suddenly Katie said, "EVP session 1. It is June 22, 2005, and it is 11:36 p.m." We turned to each other wondering what an EVP was. Then I said it cannot possibly be the year 2005. The last year I could remember was when the asylum closed in 1898. I looked at Angeline telling her these ladies must be crazy or something. Angeline just giggled.

"They are laughing, Katie," Desiree said.

How could she know what I said? Angeline told me that she had heard of people who could talk to the dead. I just smirked at her.

Katie began to ask us questions. "Can you tell us your names, please?"

Before we had a chance to respond, Desiree said the woman's name sounds like Angel but there is more to it. The boys name starts with a J, with a soft sound. Before Katie had a chance to ask us another question Angeline said, "My name is Angeline and the boy is Josiah."

"Let me get the information out that I am receiving before you ask any more questions, Katie. That way if you capture any EVPs, I will be able to validate what I am getting about them," Desiree said.

Katie agreed and waited while Desiree spouted off information she felt pertained **to** us. She said, without hesitation, "The woman was a nurse or caretaker. She watched over the children here and was a nice looking woman in life with a tender heart. The boy seems to have been a patient here; he died a tragic death. Someone killed him. Actually, the same person killed both of them. They have been here for a very, very long time. I see a man by the name of Sam being the cause of their deaths."

We were in shock. How could she know all that about us?

"We just got something, Des. My voice activation on my digital recorder just started up."

"Can you help us?" Angeline asked.

Apparently, these women did not hear her. Desiree seemed to be done for the moment and told Katie to begin to ask questions. As Katie asked questions, we answered as best we could but we wanted to get the important information out.

Suddenly Desiree said, "They seem desperate about something. I am getting that they want us to follow them." We were thrilled someone was listening.

In the hope that they would hear her, Angeline yelled, "Follow us!"

"Did you hear that?" Katie asked with her eyes widening.

Desiree nodded, "It sounded like a female voice."

Moving toward the door, Desiree told Katie that if we leave they should follow us. Desiree said there are at least 20 ghosts, probably even more. She told Katie she could feel an evil entity holding the others here.

"I think his name is Jack," Desiree said. Angeline and I just looked at each other in relief that Jack had been discovered.

Down the hall, we could see the three men with Katie and Desiree. Angeline went to the door of the area where we found the secret room with the jars and slammed the door open. I stood back, giggling, as the people all jumped from the noise. The men entered the room and noticed the second door where I found the bodies. Then they spotted the secret space beyond that. Paul was the first to enter, shining a light around the room.

"What the hell? You have got to see this," he said. Brad entered next with Jake behind him.

"Get this on video," Brad said. "We need to show this to the police. We have to research the history of this building to get some more answers."

Angeline stood close by and spoke up saying, "There is more."

"Did you guys hear a woman say something?" Jake asked.

"Yes. Was it Katie or Des? Go check, Jake," Paul said.

He left the room but returned saying they are down the hall. After pointing their machines around the room, they all agreed to move on to see what else they could find. Angeline and I walked in front of them as they looked through every ward along the way. We thought we should be with Desiree so she could talk to us some more so we went to catch up with the women.

The next area we came to was the children's ward. As they entered, Desiree looked sad, telling Katie there was a great deal of tragedy in this area.

"Children were kept here. Many children had been here over the years while this asylum was open. A lot of them died and not by natural causes. I am getting the feeling of tortures beyond belief on these poor children," Desiree said.

She appeared overwhelmed by what she saw. As she walked into Lilah's old room, she told Katie a teenage girl hung herself here. As I listened to Desiree, the memories of what happened to my friend so many years ago brought tears to my eyes. Angeline put her hand on my shoulder to comfort me.

"I know your name now—it is Josiah," Desiree said. She told Katie about how I had been kept here in this place for about three years. "I see now how he died. This is a horrible place," and she broke down. The pain of all that had happened in or around the children's ward became too much to bear.

"I have to get out of here now," she told Katie. "These children were tortured, molested and beaten regularly. Let's go. I can't take anymore."

We all left the ward and walked farther down the hall to the basement door. Katie had to give it a strong pull, but managed to get it to open. Desiree went back to find the men. After Brad's experience, and Desiree's feeling of an evil presence, they thought it best to stay together. When the men arrived, Jake led the way down the stairwell. The basement was dark and they all could feel heaviness in the air.

"We need to be really careful down here. This ghost is mean; he was the murderer of numerous children," Desiree said. They made their way carefully through the maze of rooms.

Neither Angeline nor I wanted to go back down into the basement, but we knew we had to warn them about where Jack might be. As I had done for Angeline before her death, we made noises to guide them. Finally, they reached the farthest area in the basement where they found the room. They discovered the children's clothing, shoes, hair ribbons and the bloody mattresses.

"He is in here, guys," Desiree said.

Apparently, his attack earlier drained him and he had come back to this room where he felt he was most powerful. As he crouched in the corner, Desiree said, "I can see you there and I know your name, Jack." She seemed able to see what type of person he was.

"You bastard," she shrieked. "How could you be so vile?" Jack crouched in the corner, laughing at her.

"We need to do a blessing and cleansing to bind this asshole. He killed more children over the years than I can count and he needs to go—NOW!" Desiree said.

"It won't happen," they heard a male voice say.

As they backed out of the room slowly, I could see Jack standing, his strength returning.

"I feel dizzy and sick to my stomach," Brad said.

Angeline and I did our best to get Jack's attention and keep him from harming anyone, but he lunged at Desiree. She staggered backward hitting her head on the wall. Paul ran to her asking if she was alright. She said she was fine and that was the last time that so-and-so was ever going to hurt anyone again.

"We are going to take back this place for all the spirits here. He is weak now," she said. "This is the best time to bind him so let's get to it."

As they chanted prayers, I watched Jack as he seemed to really weaken and collapse near where his body was buried. As the people moved back into the room trapping him there, he tried to run. I did not understand, but they lay salt across all the openings in the room. As he reached the salt-covered threshold, he bounced off of it like he was a ball.

When they finished praying, Jack was too weak to resist and they began to bind him. We watched as darkness surrounded him. It pulled at him until we could no longer see him. Jack was gone forever. They had sent his soul away, hopefully to hell.

We could not believe the nightmare was finally over. They still had to find all the bodies in the walls; otherwise, we felt all of us who were trapped here could never rest. To make sure, Angeline went to the wall where we found the bodies and tapped on it. They all turned when they heard the noise.

Desiree walked forward when she saw the girl's hair.

"Give me a flashlight," she said. She shined the light into the opening in the wall, finding the bodies as we had. "Oh my God," she gasped. Everyone in the group asked her what was wrong and they took turns looking as each gasped in horror. Jake found a shovel and began to knock away the bricks. Once enough of the fake wall was down, we saw hundreds of small skeletons behind it.

"Look at this. I found the skeleton of a woman, too," Brad said.

"Oh my dear Lord, that is me," Angeline whispered.

They stood silently for many minutes. I suppose they were in shock from their discovery.

"We cannot disturb this site. The police will want to see everything as it is," Brad said. So they gathered their things and quickly left the basement. Angeline and I were so thankful that, after all these years, our time of leaving this place was at hand. We felt truly blessed; the evil that had plagued us in the asylum was gone forever.

When they reached the main floor, we had to show them one last place so we banged the door leading outside and continued to make noises for them to follow us.

"Where are you taking us?" Desiree asked. "I feel they are telling us there is more we need to find." They saw the grave markers and Brad decided they should break into teams.

Brad and Jake went to look over the cemetery while the others followed us to the nearby oven building. It took them no time whatsoever to discover what we found. As they looked around, Paul noticed the journal with all the names of those who had died in the asylum. He quoted the number of deaths related to this horrid place. He said that 6,370 people are buried out there and 9,420 people were cremated.

"That cannot be possible," Katie said.

"The numbers are right here. Look for yourself," Paul said, handing her the book.

After making our way back to the building, Jake said they needed to call the police.

"These people died here for nothing and, from what we have seen, I would say 99 percent of them were murdered for their body parts. Whoever ran this place was making a profit off of the suffering of these people," Jake said.

When the police arrived, a sergeant entered the building and they showed him everything they had found. The police knew the story of Miss Dottie and her staff and were not surprised. Sgt. McCullen explained to the team that Miss Dottie and her cronies purchased people from the chief of police, Thomas Archer, who ran the operation. They were used for horrific experiments, prostitution and cadaver use for scientific study for profit.

"No one knew of the other horrors that had taken place here. What a bunch of idiots," he said, shaking his head. So what happened to Miss Dottie, Sam and Bill we wondered. Desiree told the sergeant they want to know what happened to Miss Dottie.

"Who wants to know?" he asked. She told him that two spirits who were being held there by the name of Angeline and Josiah want to know. He told them that Miss Dottie had died of old age. Sam and Bill were murdered in a prison riot. Angeline and I jumped for joy to hear that. At least they got what they deserved.

After an exhausting day, the police left with all the evidence discovered by the team. Within a short time, Desiree received a phone call from Sgt. McMullen telling her that he had researched the case and found that the names she had mentioned were absolutely correct.

"I know they were. They told me," she said. He also told her that Angeline Taylor had been a nurse sent to the asylum by the state to watch over the children and Josiah, with no last name, was a patient on the list of missing persons reported to the police by a little girl named Sarah and her grandparents.

The state police had apparently come to arrest the staff because of Angeline's mysterious disappearance. They assumed she was put into the black market operation as a prostitute and shipped out of the country, or was forced to work locally under an assumed name. No one ever questioned that it could have been a murder.

Soon after, Desiree returned to the asylum to share the whole story with us. We were happy to see her again.

"Angeline and Josiah, and the rest of you that are listening, you are free now. There is no reason for you to stay. Your story has been told and the other side awaits you. It is time to go home," she told us.

It was finally over. Quiet returned to the asylum. The building itself began to breathe. A great relief came to Angeline and me as we watched a bright light appear at the end of the hallway.

Can this be happening at last? We stood back watching people disappear into the light.

As we walked toward it, I saw Charlie, Lilah and Sarah standing in the light.

Sarah had died several years before of old age, a happy woman.

"Come on Josiah," she said, "It is your time to come home now."

"Let's go, my little friend," Angeline said, taking my hand, and we entered the light together as we had promised so many years before, never to see the asylum again.

THE END

Dark Souls

Written By: Daniel Norvell

Chapter One

Revenge

I worked late that night. I came home to a busted front door and blood all over the house. I ran into our bedroom and there, on the bed, lay the body of my wife, shot in the head.

I heard my son cry out and I turned and ran to his room. A man standing over him with a gun whipped around and squeezed the trigger. I felt the bullet rip into my stomach and exit through my back. I hit the floor in anguish.

I looked up to see the man throw a pillow over my son's face and squeeze off several rounds into my little boy. He then walked over and kicked me in the face. "That should teach you to pay your debts, you piece of shit."

I got a good look at his face as he pulled the trigger once more. I remember the gun being aimed at my face and then everything went black.

The next thing I remember is my wife and son standing in a brilliant light and my son was saying, "Daddy, come with us." The light disappeared and I remained standing in a pool of my own blood. My lifeless body lay at my feet.

I walked out of the house and the man that ended the lives of my family and me was on a cell phone. "It's done, boss. 2575 Fifth Avenue."

I could hear a voice on the other end, "You damn idiot! The address was 2575 Fifth STREET. You just killed the wrong people!"

"Well . . . I guess I made a mistake, but I don't think that guy will complain about it." The voice on the other end of the line laughed and so did the man. "I'll go and take care of it right now, boss."

The man got into an expensive looking car and drove off. I sat there on the front steps, shaking my head. My family was murdered over a mistaken address and these people couldn't care less. I was sickened and, if I still had a stomach, I would have been ill.

I walked back into my house and, by that time, the sun was rising. It appeared that this man had broken in, beat my wife and dragged her all around the house before he shot her. I was filled with anger.

I dropped to my knees and cried out, "Why God? Why did this happen? I will give my soul for revenge!"

I heard a voice behind me. "Be very careful what you wish for, Victor."

I turned and saw a man in a black cloak and hood. I couldn't see his face.

"Who are you?" I asked with a shudder.

"I am the angel of death. I am a product of heaven to perform a function. I really am not an angel, I have no allegiance to heaven or hell, I just perform a function and my function is death, no matter how it comes to people."

"So you were here just moments ago when my family was taken?"

"I was and I took your lives."

I tried to grab the man. "You rotten son of a bitch!" I screeched.

The man picked me up by the throat and I felt as if I was being choked. "Just because you are dead, does not mean that I cannot inflict pain on your soul. Calm down."

He set me down and I looked at him while rubbing my throat "Where are my wife and son?"

"They have crossed over. Your anger and hatred are keeping you here. There is nothing you can do, Victor. I returned when I heard you offer your soul. You had better be thankful it was me that heard you and not one of the devil's minions."

"And what if it were?" I asked. "Would I be able to avenge the senseless deaths of the innocent lives?"

"No. You would have been tricked into losing your soul to hell and that would serve no purpose. You have been a good man all of your life and it seems that a strange twist of fate has brought us together."

It was then and there that I struck a deal with the angel of death.

"Victor, I will grant your wish. You will work for me. The job is simple. You will see to it that people die. I have many that work with me, but your job will be special. You will kill those that have been evil. You will kill them and send them on their way to hell."

"What's the catch?" I asked.

"The catch—you will belong to me. You will do the job I assign to you and you will do it until I set you free to be with your family. That could be 100 years from now; it could be never. It will be the chance you have to take and the choice is yours."

"I'll do it under one condition. I get to be the one that kills the ones responsible for my family dying."

"Agreed. And, after that, you kill for me. You kill no matter where the soul is bound for and you kill on my command. It is an act of nature, Victor, and it will happen with or without you. Revenge will taint your soul. Be careful not to let it consume you for, if it does, your soul will have no salvation. It will find only despair in the pits of hell."

"So, I kill without the threat of going to hell?" I asked, trying to wrap my mind around the arrangement.

"You perform a necessary function, Victor. The Lord will not hold that against you. The first thing I grant you is your revenge. After that, you kill for me."

I agreed to the deal and my appearance changed. I was now wearing a black cloak of my own. I did not appear to be the same man that I was. I felt my face and there was no longer flesh on it. I looked at the man and, for the first time, he looked at me. I was staring into the face of a skeleton.

"Now you look like me, Victor. There are some rules to our game. You cannot let everyone die peacefully in their sleep. If everyone dies that way, death no longer will be feared and that fear helps to keep a number of people faithful. You will be able to use a gift I have given you—that if you think it, it will come to pass.

"So, if you want to take someone in a car accident for example, you can think of the gas pedal sticking or the brakes giving out or a heart attack behind the wheel and it will happen."

"Anything else? I have some people I need to track down," I said, impatiently.

"Patience, Victor. You now have eternity. You do not want to make it too easy on them with something quick now, do you?

"Victor, you will be seen by the deceased after you have killed them. It will be up to you to decide how you appear to them. You can look like you do now or like a nice old man, but you cannot reveal yourself before the deed is done. I will make one exception to this rule. You can reveal yourself to the man that killed you but, after that, never again before death."

"Why didn't I see you at the time of my death?" I asked.

"It is because I have made myself well accustomed to hiding in the shadows. It is time to start our work, Victor. You have to carry out your first assignment."

Chapter Two

Irony

It seemed that irony was already going to take a bite of me. The first person I was going to have to kill would be my mother.

"My mother?" I asked, incredulously."I thought I would be in charge of the people that are evil? My mother isn't evil!"

"You are correct. Your mother is not evil. But she will die this morning after hearing news of the act that took her family from her. It will be up to you to carry this out, Victor. It is the first lesson in the line of many you will come to know."

In an instant, we were in my mother's house. The phone was ringing and I knew it would be the police calling. She never answered the phone. I paced the floor in her apartment. I kept thinking, "How much misery could my sisters take? They lost me, their nephew, their sister-in-law and their mother all in one day." I didn't think I could do it.

The angel appeared. "What are you waiting for, Victor? This is what you wanted, is it not? Whether you do it or I do, your mother will die today. Remember what the rules are; they may be used to your advantage in this case."

There came a knock at my mother's door. I looked out and it was the police. My mother went to the door and the officers broke the news to her. I thought, "Heart attack."

My mother started to breathe hard and she grabbed her chest. She fell to the floor and the officers called on their radios for an ambulance. I stood and watched my mother stand up from her body and look at me. She let out a blood-curdling scream and ran into her bedroom. I remembered that I looked like death but, also, that I could appear to her as anyone.

I followed her into her room and appeared as myself. "Mom, Mom . . . it's me. I have come to show you the way to heaven."

She looked up at me. "Victor? What was that? How are you here?"

A brilliant light began to shine. "Mother, you need to go. Walk into the light. I know that Dad is waiting for you."

"You aren't coming with me?" she asked.

"I am not, Mom. I will think of you all every minute of my existence, I promise." I hugged my mother and sent her into the light.

I started to think that I had made a mistake and that I should have crossed with my family. I looked at my mother's body on the floor and watched the officers working to save her life. The angel put his bony hand on my shoulder. "Victor, you have done well. Most could not have done it. If you look at it this way, it was a gift to you from me."

"How do you figure that, you prick?" I spat through my grief.

"Name calling will not get you any points, Victor. The gift was that it could have been another and they could have made your mother suffer for a few hours. So it was your call and she went out your way. That was my gift to you."

I didn't feel as though I had received any gift. I felt completely horrible and I wondered when I would have to take the life of another I loved because of my twisted deal.

"When do I get to exact my revenge?" I asked.

"I am in charge of all deaths, Victor. He shall be yours. I promised you that and I will uphold my end of our bargain. I have a few more jobs for you to carry out, but they should be much easier for you.

"These people are Mexican drug lords. I want them to suffer before you take them, Victor. They do not deserve any mercy, for they show none."

In an instant, I was in a Mexican warehouse. I observed a number of men standing around, smoking cigars and cigarettes. They were counting money and laughing about how the man they killed last night had screamed like a pig.

All at once, I thought, "Massacre!" The Mexican police burst through the doors and opened fire. The men picked up their weapons and shot back. I walked up to one of the men, looked at him and thought, "Bullet through the head!" Instantly, a bullet hit him right between the eyes. He rose out of his body and looked at my skeletal face. He pointed and screamed. I said, "Nobody can hear you, my evil friend. You have come to meet your death!"

All at once, a black pit opened beneath the man. I am not sure what it belonged to, but the claw of what grabbed that man by the leg was a lot scarier than me, of that I was sure. That man screamed until the pit closed over the top of him. I thought to myself, "Welcome to hell, you cold hearted bastard!"

It seemed that revenge was being carried out by me and these people were as deserving as any to receive my wrath. One by one the drug lords fell. Just by a thought, they died. They would die as I saw fit—a ruptured aorta, a head shot, whatever I could think of. That is the way they went and, each time, I observed that hideous claw grab them and take them to the pits of hell.

I actually enjoyed the deaths of these evil men. I saw another hooded figure on the side of the police. He had a gentle glowing face. He would actually hold onto the hands of the victims he claimed and help them into the light. I would see him make the sign of the cross as he sent them through. After the moaning stopped and they were all dead and sent to the other side, I walked toward the other hooded figure.

"You must be the one that sends the good ones along," I said.

He looked at me with tears streaming down his face.

"Hey, I know it is horrible but it is a fact of life. Death will visit everyone," I said.

His gentle eyes rested upon my empty sockets. "I weep not for the souls that I have had to send to my Lord's kingdom, but for you. I weep for the lost soul you have become, Victor. Not even a day and the revenge that has filled you has made you enjoy the fact that the power you now possess can feed the thirst for your hopeless journey. I pity the soul that is being lost."

"Who was there to weep for my family? Who wept for my innocent little boy as a monster put bullets through his tiny head? Save your tears for a soul that deserves them! I am finding my new found power to be right where it needs to be," I responded, angrily.

The gentle-faced man looked at me. "Revenge will consume you. It will make you worse than the pit you are charged with overseeing. It will make you a brother to the Prince of Darkness himself. Do not let that happen, Victor. You may once again be reunited with that little boy, but not if revenge takes the place of the soul of the good man you once were."

"I will not be ashamed of the feeling it gives me to end the life of someone that deserves it. I will be the best dealer of death that I can be when it comes to taking evil people to meet in hell," I told him.

"Then maybe you are already there yourself, Victor. May God protect the soul you have left."

He was gone and I looked around at the carnage. I felt my face crack as I smiled, "They deserved it." I looked forward to the next group of evil that I would be able to introduce myself to and I began to almost pity them. I pity them because I would become very good at the job I was given. It was the best job I had ever had and I would do it until I was able to meet, face-to-face, the man that had taken everything from me. What a glorious day that would be.

I found myself in the apartment of a man in New York City. He had just finished cutting the arm off of a girl he had just strangled and was drinking her blood! I looked at her little face. She couldn't have been more than 10. The way in which I would take out this lowlife would be terrible, even to the angel that gave me the job.

Chapter Three

Show No Mercy

I watched the man drink the blood of that little girl and then start to eat her flesh. I was sickened by the fact that the Lord above would allow such a miserable creature access to our world. What pissed me off even more was that the police would never find this girl; the family would never have a body to place at rest. I thought about the most horrific ways to end him.

What could I do to make him suffer? I thought, "Take your own life!" "Take scissors and cut your leg to the bone. Eat on your own flesh until you bleed out."

The man stopped what he was doing and got up to find scissors. He placed the scissors to his leg and he began to cut. He cut until I could see his bone. As he cut, he peeled his flesh off and started to eat it. I actually stopped him and thought, "Stick the scissors into your heart." The man stopped, turned the scissors toward himself, and thrust as hard as he could into his own heart. I heard him gasp a few times and fall from his chair. I would reveal the true face of fear as he rose from his body. The man wriggled around and finally died. He rose and looked at me.

"Who are you?"

"I was sent here to make sure that you hurt nobody else. I was sent here to make sure you died."

I stood there and stared at him. I was waiting for the pit to open but it did not. Why wasn't this man going to hell?

"Where are you going to take me?"

I wasn't sure how to answer him. I had never seen this happen before. The door of the house opened and another man walked in with grocery bags.

"Shit!" he started yelling. "That little prick got loose and started without me!"

It hit me: I had killed the wrong man! This was a sick man who was being tortured by the other man. That had to be the reason that the man I was standing with did not cross. I looked at the man I had just killed.

"Is this what you wanted to do?" I asked him.

"No. Harold told me to drink and eat the little girl to get rid of her body. He went to the store to get things to cook her with. I didn't want to do it, but he said he would kill me if I didn't. I was scared so I started before he returned."

I felt pain inside my head and the angel appeared. "Victor, you have dispatched an innocent soul. You have shown no mercy in it and you now owe me one soul."

I watched the angel of death walk over and say, "Surprise!" to the other man. The man turned and looked. He screamed as the angel ripped his heart from his chest. The man fell to the ground. As he rose from his body, the angel grabbed him from his hair. "I now condemn you to hell!" A pit opened beneath the man and the angel threw him into it.

The angel walked over, grabbed the man that I had killed and threw him in, as well. "I have no use for a moronic ghost walking around this earth. Victor, you have made a mistake that will cost you dearly.

"You have let revenge consume you. You did not provide a function, but provided judgment. It is not up to us to judge anyone. We kill who we are supposed to. You killed an innocent person. One that was to live and make a difference by being studied for mental illness. That won't happen now."

"I am sorry. I didn't know. I made a mistake."

"Similar to the mistake that took your life. Victor? It was not malice that killed your family; it was a mistaken address. I do not agree with the fact that your family was taken, but you have just committed the very same act, so to speak."

The angel looked at me with those empty eye sockets. "You now owe me a soul. I do not care where it comes from and I do not care how long it takes. You also will not be allowed to enact your revenge on the man that killed you. This is the soul that I will take in payment for the one you owe me."

"You sent me here on half-truths and bullshit. You knew damn well that I would dispatch that man and you did nothing to stop it. You said that you are in control of all deaths; that is how I know you lied to me."

"I told you to be careful what you wished for, Victor! I told you that you would be in charge of killing evil people. Who do you really think you are working for? You have made a deal with the devil, Victor, and those deals are not easily broken. Everyone that you kill is another soul for me.

He continued. "I have accepted your payment and I will stand by my end of the bargain. You will stay in my service and continue to kill until the man that killed you dies and I have his soul in my possession. Then, if God will have you, he can. If he won't, you can either wander the earth, or continue the grisly job I have given you. I will spare you the fire and pit of hell."

"So you are the devil."

"I am not. I am the one that finds hapless souls and I talk them into working for the darkness. I answer to him and you answer to me so, in all reality I suppose, to you I am the devil."

I could not understand why the angel at the drug lords' warehouse had not told me this. Maybe he tried and I didn't listen. I looked back at the devil's minion, "So I cannot kill the man that killed me and I am not free until he dies. Right?"

"You are correct, Victor."

I had the information I needed. I would return after the man that killed me was dead.

"Victor, I have another job for you."

"Keep it I have one of my own," I replied. I walked out of that apartment to look for the man that killed my family.

Chapter Four

Revenge Comes With a Price

I searched for days for the man that had killed us. I finally caught up with him as he was getting ready to throw a body into the Hudson River. I walked close to him. "Hey!" I yelled.

The man looked around wildly. "Who said that!? Who is out here messing with me?"

"Remember the family you killed? The ones that lived at the address you screwed up on?"

The man turned white as a sheet. "I killed you, man! I killed you dead!"

"You killed innocent people. I am sure we were not the first, but the body on the ground in front of you will be your last!"

The man jumped into his car and sped off, leaving the body lying there.

"Now the police will find the body and if I am to spend the rest of his life waiting, I'm OK with it," I thought to myself. I found it easy to follow the man. No matter how fast he drove, he could not lose me. I sat in the passenger seat of the car.

"Can you feel the hands of revenge tightening around your throat?"

The man let out a scream. "Why are you haunting me?!"

"I am not leaving your side until you see my face at the time of your death!"

The man slammed the gas pedal to the floor. "Get away from me!" he screamed.

"No. I am going to stick to you until you take your last breath," I said.

The man drove faster and faster until he lost control of the car and slid under a semi trailer. The car collapsed like a can being smashed. I stood outside of the car as the man that killed my wife, my little boy and myself struggled to take his last breaths. I turned away as the man's soul rose from the wreckage. I didn't want him to see my face yet.

"Turn and face me, you prick!" the man said.

I turned and he gasped as he stared into my empty eye sockets. I looked into his face. "Welcome to hell. They'll be here in a second."

The pit began to open under the man's feet and the claw I had seen many times before grabbed the man by the leg. He screamed loudly as the claw tightened around his leg and he began to catch fire.

"Goodbye. I hope eternity keeps you warm," I said.

The man disappeared into the puddle of blackness. The angel that had recruited me to this grisly job appeared.

"I told you that his soul would make us even, but you killed him. The deal is nullified."

"I could give a shit less what you do to me now, you freak. Do what you will."

In an instant, my flesh returned to my body. "I will grant you your flesh back so that it may burn in the pit I will condemn you to."

"I'm waiting," I responded, smiling.

Nothing happened.

"Master! Take him now. He has broken his end of the bargain. He killed the man that took his life," he cried.

I looked into the emptiness of the angel's eye sockets.

"I did not take his life. I simply watched as he died in an accident that I had nothing to do with. It was not my doing if he could not handle being haunted by the man he killed."

The angel came at me and grabbed for my throat. "There are fates worse than the death you suffered!" I felt his bony hands tighten around my throat. I felt my feet come off of the ground and a voice from behind me said, "Put him down!"

The angel dropped me. "Master, he has betrayed me. He should pay. He went against the contract."

I turned to see a man dressed in a black suit; his eyes were completely black.

"You are the one that betrayed the contract. You tricked him into killing an innocent and then you tried to use this act to seal his soul as yours. All souls in hell are mine!"

With a wave of his hand, the angel started to sink into a black puddle like the ones I had seen others sink into. The angel screamed in pain as he sank and then he was gone.

I knew at that instant that I was in the presence of the devil himself. He looked at me. "He has served me for 400 years. He brought me every evil soul you can ever think of. I cannot replace him easily."

"I am not sure what you are going to do, but I will take eternal damnation before I will take another life in your name."

"I have no intention of damning you or making you take any more lives," he replied with a smile. "I do not let souls in my employ make their own rules. That is up to me. I grant your soul back to you and your contract is fulfilled."

I couldn't believe what I heard. I didn't know whether to thank him or run.

"Where will I go?" I asked.

"You will go wherever the Lord of Heaven decides for you to go. I will tell you this, however. You have killed with revenge in your heart. The Lord may not be able to see clear of that. You may end up with me anyway."

An angel, more beautiful than I could have ever imagined, appeared and a brilliant light surrounded him.

"Michael, I did not think you would come here yourself," the black-suited man said to the angel.

"I am only here because you are here, Lucifer. You need to go now. The Lord has granted you your moment here. Leave and do not return again."

"If I do see you again, you will be made to kill again. I need to replace my loss and you have already proven you are effective. Farewell for now," Lucifer said to me before melting into a black puddle.

"You have been placed into a very sad situation. You were taken before your time and you watched your family taken, as well. Unfortunately, you will only remember them the way you saw them last. The Lord forgives you for what it was that you were tricked into doing and that is not the reason you will not be allowed into his kingdom.

"The reason that you will not be allowed in is because you thought of nothing but revenge. The angel of heaven told you this, he even wept for you, and you did not heed his warning."

"I beg for your mercy. I will accept the penance that the Lord has instructed you to give me," I said, falling to my knees before him.

"The Lord instructed me to look for hope. I looked into your heart and found none," he responded, looking deeply into my eyes.

"You are happy that the man died in the car. You are happy that, indirectly, you are responsible."

"I am. I cannot deny it," I responded, my eyes downcast.

"That is why I cannot take you with me. I wish I could, but it cannot be. We had hoped that you would not let revenge taint your soul, but it has. If that darkness is allowed into our Father's realm, it will no longer be heaven and the purity of the soul will leave.

"You must be sorry and repent for your sins. You have repented, but you are not sorry and that is why you will stay here."

"Stay here?"

"Yes. You will be the spirit that can be heard by those planning revenge. Revenge is never the answer and the Father wants you to help those like you before they suffer the same fate. You will be protected from Lucifer and his minions, but you will remain here to perform this task until you truly figure out what it means to chase revenge from your heart.

"I hope that you do some day," he said, sadly.

That was the last time that I spoke with an angel. I have helped many people to change the error of their ways with the gift that the angel has bestowed upon me. I have a feeling that I will perform this task for a long time to come because, to be honest, I can never feel remorse for knowing that the man that killed my family is burning in hell and I am the one that chased him there.

Even though I have not been damned by the Lord, I have damned myself. I cannot forget the savage act toward my family and I cannot forget the coldness that the man displayed while taking my son's life in front of me.

The last memory of my wife and son were not so bad. They were standing in a light and I know that they are with our Lord. It does not make it easier, but it does make it tolerable. I will never forget them and the hell I suffered when I witnessed them die. I will repay my debt to humanity and I will try to save every soul I can from the same fate as mine.

THE END

The Journal of Clyde Tucker

Written By: Sandy Wells

Story Collaboration: Russ Wells

Chapter One

Wandering!

The drought had become severe; finding water was difficult. As I woke up that morning, I found my only blanket covered in dust from the storm the night before. I had often wondered when these storms would ever subside. Every day since I had lost my job on the farm near the small community of Manor, I had been wandering throughout Oklahoma looking for some kind of work, but most towns I had come to had signs posted that no jobs were available and that transients were not welcome. How did those people expect someone like me to ever find a way to eat and survive without a chance to work? Every day was a struggle to find food; I usually ate about once a day. I never was able to find enough to fill my belly, though. Oftentimes I thought of how lucky I was to have a strong back and was able to work. Many times I thought about if I had this much trouble finding food for just myself, how hard it must have been for families trying to feed their children. It made me sad to think about how this country had gone so wrong for so many.

As I wandered around the state, I would see tent cities full of families. From time to time, I would stop to do some trading for food. Each person had stories of how they ended up on the road, from losing a business to foreclosures of their homes or farms. Even though I was only 24 years old, it felt as if I had heard it all before. Today as I walked into a camp of three men sitting on the side of the road, I said "Hey men, can you spare a cup of joe? How are you doing? My name is Clyde." These men were very quiet; one of them looked up at me saying his name was Eddie Colter. The other two did not say their names, which I thought rather odd but I guess it was not important. They did not seem to be very friendly but gave me the cup of coffee anyway. I told them thanks, drank down the coffee and was on my way. For no particular reason, I felt very uncomfortable being around them but I thought it was just because the issue of trust did not come easily these days. Being cautious during these trying times had become the normal way of life for most folks. I had heard stories of murders for no other reason than a piece of food. Of the three men I had encountered a short time ago, Eddie Colter gave me the most uneasy feeling. I was glad to be away from them and knew the chance of meeting them again was not likely.

Continuing down the road, I began my search for a place to lay my head for the night. It had to be a place that was quite a ways off the road. I had learned from personal experience that you were safer not being by any road. I recently had some of what little belongings I had stolen while I was asleep. It was extremely lucky that I had awakened at all, to be honest. I had one of my blankets taken but it was coming into spring now so I figured they must have needed it more than I did.

Every night before laying my head down, I would write down my experiences of the day. I thought of myself as an aspiring writer and hoped to share some of mine and others' experiences of the Great Depression and its hardships in a book. That was my dream. I had no family to speak of since my parents had died in 1930 at the onset of the Depression. It had happened in a car accident quite unexpectedly when I was 20. That is when I realized it was up to me to forge my own future the best that I could.

The next day when I woke up, the sky was full of clouds that had almost a reddish hue to them. As I looked across the landscape of the area, it was as if someone had placed a wall to hide my view. Then I noticed that this wall of what looked like rolling and bubbling clouds extending to the ground seemed to be getting closer. Suddenly, I realized it was an intense dust storm. I hurried to find my blanket and wrap it securely around me, leaving a space for a pocket of air. I dipped my handkerchief into some water I had and tied it around my nose and mouth so I could continue to breathe until the storm had passed. These storms were becoming a more frequent occurrence. If you did not prepare yourself, a person could easily suffocate within minutes. As I sat against the tree, I waited for what seemed to be hours for the storm to subside. When it finally did, I lowered the blanket to take a look around and saw nothing but what looked like a covering everywhere of grays and browns. It was if the whole world had been painted. I shook out my blanket that had been piled with dust and gathered my things to begin my daily journey. I knew I was getting close to a river so I made that my goal for the day. I hoped to catch some fish to make a meal for myself.

Finally, after walking for some time, I could see a bridge in the distance. What a great sight to see, I thought. It had been a very long day and since I had not seen a soul on the road to do any trading for food, my stomach was quite empty and growling. Once I reached the bridge, I saw an encampment of several families with children set up near the sand bars of the river. Ladies were washing clothes, the men were fishing and the children were playing. I sat down on the bank to take in some normal scenes of how life used to be.

My mind drifted back to the days of my own childhood in Stone Water. My friends and I would play for hours making up stories of daring sword fights and rescuing damsels in distress. A smile came to my face; it had been a long time since I had those great memories. Once I snapped out of the daydream of days gone by, I figured I better go down to the encampment and speak with the men about fishing alongside them. I walked up to a fairly young man, I would say in his 30s, and I introduced myself.

"Hello sir. My name is Clyde Tucker and I was wondering if I could share your fishing hole with you and the others," I said with a smile.

"Howdy, young man. My name is Rudy. You are more than welcome to set up a campsite here with us," he replied.

I was so thankful that I could stop walking for a least a couple days. I began building myself a makeshift shack to spend my nights. Even though it may sound silly, I was happy about actually having some protection from the weather. I figured a temporary roof was better than none. I spent the rest of my day fishing with two other men on the banks of the river and actually caught a pile of fish that everyone shared. The women in the camp fried the fish in cornmeal and it was delicious. I had not had a meal like that since I had begun my wanderings about a year before. With my stomach full, I found myself getting quite sleepy and bid everyone good night. I crawled onto my blanket and fell asleep instantly.

Chapter Two

Fun Filled Day No More

Gosh, I slept well, I thought as I sat up to stretch. I guess it was all that great fish last night and a full stomach. As I stepped out of the shack, I could smell the aroma of food cooking on the open fire near the tents of the families there. I did not want to intrude on their breakfast so I began to walk the other way. Suddenly, I heard Rudy yell for me to come over to the fire. I did not want to but I always did my best to be polite like my grandmother had taught me.

As I approached, I could hear the family talking over the plans for the rest of the week. Rudy was telling his wife, Evelyn, that he had heard they were hiring men for a factory in Oklahoma City. He asked if I would like to go along and maybe get a job there, too. I told him that would be wonderful and we all sat down to a breakfast of hot mush and a small piece of ham. Rudy continued to tell me about what they did at the factory and I was actually beginning to have some hope again. Wandering around the state for as long as I had was educational, but I was tired of being without a proper home.

Once we finished our breakfast, I helped the children gather up the plates and thanked Evelyn for the meal. She just smiled in a meek way and continued doing her mending. I supposed with five children, ranging in age from 2 to 10, it must be hard to keep their clothes clean and repaired. The children were making plans with the other children in the camp to play games so I walked down by the river to do some fishing for my dinner. To be honest, I was not used to being around small children and needed a break from the constant questions and chatter. As I sat there on the log, Amanda, Rudy's eldest daughter, came up to sit and count before she had to go seeking out the others. Finally done, she ran off. After she left, I walked farther down the riverbank to get some peace and quiet. Nearly the rest of my day was spent thinking about the possible job opportunity. Just the thought of having a chance to have a home again was inspiring.

Later in the afternoon, I happened to glance up by the bridge to see Eddie Colter and the two men I had encountered a couple days earlier standing there staring down at all that was going on.

I can't really explain why, but when I saw them it was like I had been kicked in the stomach by a mule. A horrible feeling came over me, as if I knew something bad would be coming our way. They did not see me but they seemed to be very interested in the goings on at the camp. I watched closely as they came down the bank. They stopped by Rudy's tent where his wife was working on her mending, speaking with her for some time until Rudy approached. I am not sure what was said between them but Rudy and a couple other men from the camp seemed to take a defensive stance, as if they expected a fight. It looked to me that Eddie Colter seemed to have a big interest in watching the children as they played. That concerned me a great deal. Pretty much as soon as they came, they left and we all watched as they made their way over the bridge and finally out of sight.

That night for some reason, it was very important to me to write the events of that day in my journal. I guess it was just the strange feelings I got when I saw those men again. It was probably nothing, I thought; just my imagination. After I wrote in my journal that night, I fell fast asleep. Around 4 a.m., I woke to the sounds of running and a murmured child's voice. I crawled out of the makeshift door and stood up. I could not see anything, it was so dark. Then as I looked beneath the bridge, I noticed what looked like a match being struck and then the light from someone puffing on a cigarette so I made my way toward it. As quietly as possible, I got closer but by the time I reached the spot where I had seen the light, it was gone. Stumbling across the rocks under the bridge, I tripped over something on the ground. I grabbed a match from my pocket and struck it. As I looked down, I saw Amanda lying on the ground in a pool of blood. With shaking hands, I reached down to see if she was breathing. She wasn't. Her face and clothes were covered with blood. The dress or nightgown she had been wearing had been nearly ripped from her body. "Oh my God! No, not this poor child," I screamed.

While checking for sign of life, I unknowingly got her blood on my clothes and hands. Suddenly, out of the darkness came the men from the camp with Rudy leading the way.

"You son of a bitch! What have you done to my girl?" Rudy growled. Then he grabbed me and began to hit me repeatedly in the face. As I lay on the ground trying to guard my face with my hands, the other men snatched me up and pointed a revolver at me.

In the meantime, Rudy tried to revive Amanda but it was too late. I kept yelling at them that I would not harm that child. I tried to explain what happened but they would not listen to me. Rudy covered Amanda's body with a blanket and said he needed to leave her there for the police to get the evidence they needed to fry my ass in the chair. He sent one of the men ahead to drive to the police station in the town about 10 miles away.

"Please, Rudy. I did not kill her. I swear," I pleaded. No one would listen. They shoved a rag in my mouth so I could not talk and dragged me across the rocks back to the tents where they tied me up and threw me to the ground. How was I ever going to prove that I did not kill her? No one except me saw that light below the bridge. I figured the police would listen to me so maybe I still had a chance to prove my innocence. It was my only hope.

When the sun came up that morning, I saw the car drive over the bridge. It had two men in it with a big star on the side so I knew the police were coming. As soon as they walked to where I was lying, I could hear them talking to Rudy. He took them to where Amanda's body was and I could see them pointing and talking about me. When they returned to the camp, one of the officers untied me and pulled the gag from my mouth. "You are going to fry for this, young man."

I could not believe they did not even give me the chance to explain what happened. He slapped handcuffs on me and dragged me up the hill to the waiting police car. Another vehicle was sitting on the road. It looked like what we always called a meat wagon so I assumed they were there to collect Amanda's body. As the officer threw me into the back seat, he said, "We don't put up with any baby killers." I turned to look into his face, again claiming my innocence.

"You expect me to believe you? You are covered with that child's blood," the other officer replied and that was the end of the conversation. I knew my only hope would be the judge once I went to court.

God help me, I thought. I gave up and turned so I could look out the window. It did not take long for us to reach town. As we pulled up, I wondered if that would be the last time I would see anything as a free man. The officers pulled me from the back seat and walked me into the jail, where a guard removed my restraints and took me to a waiting cell. He looked at me once to say, "We have no tolerance in this state for scum like you, boy. You will see the judge in the morning." As he walked away, I heard him mumble, "Well, this one should not take long." Then he kind of chuckled as if he knew exactly what the judge would do to me.

The next morning, I was so stiff and sore from being beaten by Rudy, dragged across rocks and up the hill that I could barely move. I stood up to move around the best I could and noticed a guard stop by my cell door. "Come on," he said. "It is time to go see the judge." He laughed and added, "You better hope that Judge Hacker is in a good mood. Nothing he hates worse than a person who takes another's life, especially a child's." As the guard walked me into the courtroom, I was still in my bloody clothes from the night before. They had not even allowed me to bathe or change. As I stood in front of the bench, I looked around to see who was in the courtroom. No one was present other than who I thought was the lawyer for the state. Judge Hacker entered the courtroom and took his seat behind the bench. He just glared at me.

"What is the evidence against this man?" he asked. The lawyer began to tell the judge what they believed. The judge again glared at me as if he could see right through to my backbone. My knees were knocking and my heart raced. The story he told about what I had supposedly done was a real fabrication.

"Mr. Tucker, you have been accused of murder. Is there anything you would like to say before I pass judgment?" he said.

"Yes sir, there is. I did not kill that girl," I said and I continued on, telling him what actually happened.

"Do you have any witnesses that could corroborate your version of the story?" the judge asked.

"No, sir, I don't," I responded.

"Mr. Tucker, I have no remorse for what I am about to say. You are hereby sentenced to death row at Choctaw Penitentiary, where you will remain until your execution for the murder of Amanda Riley. May God have mercy on your soul because I feel no mercy for you."

With that, I felt my knees buckle. I could not believe what I heard. How could he convict me without a trial for a crime I did not commit? To be honest, I understood their anger and hatred for a man who would rape and murder a child, but I did not do it. I was a young man who had the rest of his life to live, but I was soon to die for a crime I did not commit.

Chapter Three

The Choctaw Mile

When I arrived at the Choctaw Mile (death row), I was stripped naked and hosed down with a high pressure hose. Once clean, they issued me a set of striped clothes to wear. I heard one guard say to the other guards, "This is the baby killer, men." I felt like such trash I knew I was an innocent man. Somehow, before they killed me, I had to prove my innocence. Suddenly, I thought of my journal. What I had written about the three men might be the proof I needed to cause reasonable doubt that I committed this murder. How was I ever going to get my journal for that proof? It was hopeless. I was going to die.

The mile had 10 men awaiting the same fate as myself. The guards ignored us most of the time. The rules were pretty simple. No talking to the guards or the other prisoners. I guess they wanted us all to be silent because that way they would not have to listen to our whining about being there. The next morning during count, I heard the black man across from me try to talk to the guard. The guard began yelling at him and then called for the door to be opened on E7. As soon as the door slid open, the guard began to beat him senseless, saying, "You are not going to make it to your execution, boy." Why were they so cruel to him? Wasn't dying in the electric chair enough for them? What else could they possibly take from us?

The beating lasted for a couple minutes then the guard stood above the man gloating at what he had done. The guard stepped out of the cell but left the prisoner lying on the floor, bleeding. I could not say a word. It would do me no good to end up like that. So I went back to sitting on my bunk pondering what little time I had left. The mile had several guards; most were alright but a few of them had no conscience. I silently thought that they needed to be in here instead of me.

One day, as they woke us, I heard the outer door open and close. Then I saw a man in a suit, very-well kept in his attire. I assumed it must be the warden.

He handed the captain a piece of paper. The guard looked at him saying, "So, it is Joe's time, huh?" Who was Joe, I thought? Then I heard one of the guard's footsteps coming toward my end of the mile. As he walked past, he glared at me to mind my own business so I sat back down on my bunk. He walked to the last cell, E10, and handed the paper to the man inside.

"That is your D.O.E., Joe. Two days left."

What does D.O.E. mean, I thought. Later, I learned it means "Date Of Execution". I began to think that all the men on the Choctaw Mile had been put here before me so maybe that meant they would go before me. I hoped it worked that way; no guarantees, I supposed. The day of Joe's execution came and the guards were busy preparing for his death that night. None of us saw them much that day so it gave us all time to whisper and talk to each other for once.

The black man across from me asked, "Why you here?" I told him what they had accused me of but that I was innocent. He just laughed. I asked him why are you laughing, it is not funny; I am going to die. He said, "I am not laughing at you, boy. I am here because they said I raped a young white woman. That's an instant death sentence."

"Did you do it?" I asked. He looked me straight in the eyes and said no. For some reason, I knew he was telling the truth. A man in E6 piped up, "Yeah, yeah, we are all innocent in here."

I am not sure where it came from but I said, "Shut your face, you ass," and continued to speak with the black man whose name was Hank. I asked if he had received his D.O.E. He said yes, but it has been put off for two more weeks. I did not want to upset him so I stopped asking questions. The torture of knowing when you were being put to death was bad enough. I became very depressed and sat down on my bunk to rest.

That night, at about 11:30, the guards came to collect Joe for his execution. Three guards surrounded Joe as he shuffled along in his shackles. He happened to glance up and look at me. I could see the fear in his eyes and a sudden feeling of dread came over me. I knew that soon it would be me walking that last few steps to my death. As I sat there, I examined my own mortality. I began to think of what I had learned about death in Sunday school as a child. Would God allow me into heaven? Would he know of my innocence or would I spend the rest of eternity in hell? I became very scared. Suddenly, the lights began to dim and brighten again. Hank looked at me and said, "It's over."

I found out very quickly that it was not a good sign to see Warden Johnston show up on the mile. He always delivered the D.O.E papers himself to the guards so when I saw him about two days later with a paper in hand, I knew someone was about to have a very bad day. As I heard the keys of the guard jingle and the footsteps getting closer, I wondered who was next. I expected him to walk by any moment and then I looked up to see him standing in front of my cell. He said, "Hey, baby killer. Looks like you made quite an impression on the judge." He had a smirk on his face as he shoved his arm through the bars with the D.O.E paper in his hand. "Come get it," he said.

I got up from my bunk to go grab the paper. As I looked down and read the date, I looked up to see a smile on the guard's face as if he really was going to enjoy killing me. I stepped back just shaking my head in disbelief. The date on the paper was the very next day. "Sir, I know I am not supposed to talk to you but I need to know. Why so quickly?" I asked.

"You are the killer and rapist of a child."

Do you honestly think anyone gives a Damn how quickly you die?" he growled.

"I suppose not," I said. As he walked away I thought to myself, well this is it.

That night, as I lay on my bunk, I dosed off and had a dream. In my dream, Amanda came to me saying, "I know the truth, Mr. Tucker. Don't be afraid. It will all be over soon." She told me who had killed her. She said it was the man they called Eddie and that it was a revenge killing for her father not giving him the food they asked for that day. She told me everything that happened that night. They came into the children's tent and snatched her out of bed with their hands tightly around her mouth so she could not scream. Then they carried her beneath the bridge, keeping her gagged so she could not scream for help. She told me that Eddie ripped her nightgown from her body while the other two men held her down.

"He climbed on top of me and hurt me badly and, when he got done, he picked up a large rock and dropped it hard on my head. That is all I can remember," she said. "You needed to know the truth," she said, as she slipped away back into a bright light that seemed to surround her.

The dream startled me and I jumped up from my bed. The rest of the night I sat in contemplation as to what she could have meant by me needing to know the truth. How would I ever tell someone the truth? I decided it did not matter anymore because about 12 hours from then, I would be dead.

Chapter Four

The Execution of Clyde Tucker

The rest of the night, I sat on my bunk, wide awake, wondering why Amanda would come to me. My biggest question was how did she come to me? I never really thought about death much before, but now it was a stark reality staring me in the face. The minutes were ticking by so quickly. I wish I had someone who could answer all my questions but I was alone. I prayed to God that he would take me into his kingdom and forgive me for my sins. I know this may sound crazy to people that have faith, but I have often wondered so many things about heaven and hell. Are they real or do they just exist in our mind? What happens to us when we die? Will the questions I am asking myself about faith in God condemn me to hell?

I guess faith is not as easy as many make it out to be. I cannot believe that I am the only one who has questions like these. As I sat there listening to the sounds of the quiet around me, I was still in disbelief that by today at a certain time I would no longer exist. Clyde Tucker, the person, would be dead. I had heard stories of relatives coming to take me to heaven when I die. Was this true? I wondered. I hope so. The only comfort I knew was that this nightmare would soon be over.

It must be 6 a.m. because the lights just came on in the mile. I began to hear movement by the guards. I am really glad I will not have to listen to the jingling of their keys much longer. It was beginning to drive me crazy. I think they do that just to irritate the prisoners. I walked up to my cell door to see one of the guards stop in front of me. He said, "What do you want for your last meal tonight before it happens?"

"I don't care; does it really matter?"

"Fine. You don't have to take anything special," he said.

I just looked at him and said, "I am not hungry anyway; would you be?"

He just shook his head and walked away. After they passed out morning chow, two of the guards came up to my cell saying they had to prepare me for tonight. The guard Ralph, who seemed to be a decent man, said, "We have to shave the top of your head now."

"Why?" I asked.

He told me that it was so that they could make a good electrical connection to my skin. I was so despondent that I just said, "Sure, why not."

As they shaved my head, I knew my time was getting closer. My insides were shaking. The fear of death was becoming more real to me. This was not a nightmare that I would be able to wake from. After they finished, they walked out and closed the door behind them. Even though I was not fond of any of the guards, I wished that one of them would stay and talk to me. I wished my mom was here with me. I am a kid, for God's sake. Why is this happening to me? I began to get angrier by the minute. The rage I felt for how I had been railroaded into this position became so overwhelming that I could no longer contain it. I began to cry out about my contempt of everything I had been through in the last week or so.

Suddenly, I heard and could see the guards running toward me. "Do you not understand me? Can no one hear what I have said? I did not kill that girl!" As they opened the cell door, three of the largest guards began to pull at me and push me to the floor. Once there, I began to struggle and fight them the best I could but to no avail. They forced me into a straight jacket to restrain me. I kept yelling, "I did not kill Amanda Riley! Please, don't kill me. Please, please." As they stood me on my feet, Ralph looked me in the eyes, telling me to calm down.

"I don't understand why this is happening to me. I am innocent. I need to talk to someone so I can prove my innocence," I said.

"It is too late for that," Ralph said.

"Are you kidding me? I do not deserve to die."

"Calm down," Ralph said. His voice was actually quite supportive and nurturing. With tears in my eyes, I began to relax. I don't want to die. God, please help me. I actually felt as if my mind was slipping away. They left me sitting on my bed in the jacket. I guess they did not want me to hurt myself. How ironic, I thought. Of course I would not want to deny the state their murder, I thought.

As they stood in the open area between the cells, I could hear Ralph talking to the other guards. "Do you think this boy is telling the truth about his innocence? Something is just not right here. Could the judge have made a mistake?"

One of the other guards said, "It is very strange, without a doubt. There is nothing we can do for him; the D.O.E. is set. It happens in two hours."

"I need to talk to Warden Johnston now," Ralph said. I heard the outer door open and close. As I sat there praying for a miracle, I hoped Ralph would be that miracle that could save me. It seemed he had been gone for some time when I heard the outer door open and close again.

I could hear voices but not what they were talking about. What had he found out, I wondered. The clock was ticking. I had less than one hour before they killed me. What was happening? Finally, Ralph came to my cell door. "The warden is calling the governor to see if we can get a stay of execution for you. There is no guarantee, Clyde," Ralph said.

"Thank you so much for at least listening to me. You are a nice man," I said.

"I hope this works, my boy. I just want you to know that I believe you are innocent. I am praying we are not too late. You must understand, Clyde. We hear that statement all the time from these guys, but you were different. I could see the pain in your eyes and I just knew you were telling the truth," Ralph said.

Suddenly, the phone rang and Ralph turned to answer it. I could hear him talking to someone saying, "Are you sure we can't stop this, Warden?" After a pause, he said, "I understand, sir." My heart sank because I knew it was bad news. Ralph hung up the phone and walked back over to me. "I am sorry, Clyde.

The governor's office staff can not get hold of the governor. They are continuing to try but it is not looking good."

"I have finally accepted my fate, Ralph. You have done all you can. At least you listened to me when no one else would. Thank you."

"Do not give up yet," he said. As I looked up at the clock, I could see that if nothing happened, I would be in the electric chair in less than 20 minutes. I resigned my fate and my life to God. I left it up to Him; I no longer had a choice, I thought.

It was time. The guards came into the cell and took me out of the jacket and placed shackles around my wrists and ankles. Ralph and the other guards did not say a word to me. I guess it was because they had nothing to say to make me feel any better for what was about to happen. As they slowly walked me down the final hall into the room where the execution would take place, I glanced up to see Rudy and his wife, Evelyn, sitting there staring at me. Their faces were emotionless. I could not look at them nor could I blame them for putting me here. Bad circumstances sealed my fate. The only person to blame was the man who really killed Amanda. I had no doubt who that was but it was too late. He would go free for his crime.

They sat me in the chair, strapped me down, placed a black hood over my head, and then they connected electrodes to my head, legs and arms. I began to shake uncontrollably as the guard was speaking to me. His voice echoed in my head as I heard him finally say, "May God have mercy on your soul." Then I heard, "Roll on two" and I felt an instant surge of pain, my body twitched back and forth, and everything went black.

Suddenly, I found myself standing beside the chair. As I looked around, I could see everyone sitting there staring straight ahead. What in the heck were they looking at, I wondered. As I turned and glanced down, I saw me sitting in the chair with a doctor hovering over me, listening to my heart. He slowly raised his head and nodded to Ralph. My body was slumped over in the chair so I assumed he was confirming that I was dead. I began to wonder how this was possible. How could I be standing here if my body was there in that chair? I did not understand it. As I stood there watching them taking the restraints off of my body and putting me on a table on wheels, I wondered, now what?

Ralph started to leave the room when I heard the phone on the wall ring. He walked over to it and said, "E Block." I am not sure who he was talking to but I heard him say, "No sir. It is too late. It is done." Then I heard him say, "Are you telling me that the stay has been ordered by the governor?" He lowered his head in disbelief. "Alright, sir. We will take care of it," and he hung up.

Apparently the warden had convinced the governor that something was wrong with my case and wanted it further investigated. As I stood there listening, I could not believe it . . . I did not have to die. At least I was free. As the people filed out of the execution room, I followed them. I knew that I had something to do and a place I needed to go. Regardless of whether I died or not, I had to make sure Eddie Colter paid for his crimes.

I was not sure how I did it but, somehow, I got as far as the road because I was standing in the middle of it. Very strange, I thought and began to walk back to where this started.

Chapter Five

Learning About Death

How I got there so quickly I don't know, but I found myself back at the bridge. I actually began to think of how interesting this dead thing really was. It was almost as if I could close my eyes and think where I wanted to be and, poof, I was there. Incredible, I thought. The families had moved on and nothing was left behind except my makeshift shack. The funny thing was, I had no regrets about being dead; it was almost a relief. I felt energized and so light on my feet. It was great! I did not feel hungry or tired anymore. I had the freedom to go where I wanted with no worries about food or money. Then I thought I better get to the task at hand, which was looking for my journal. It had to be here. As I crawled into the shack, I saw it lying on the ground with the rest of my things. I was happy to see it was still where I had left it. All I knew was that somehow, some way, I had to get this in a living person's hands so they could tell others about what I said that day about the three men, especially Eddie Colter. As I sat down on my blanket, I began to read through the journal about what my life had been for the year prior to my execution.

I am not really sure how long I sat there, but I crawled out to see car after car driving across the bridge. That was odd, I thought, because there had been no traffic before. As I looked around, I noticed that there was snow on the ground but I did not feel cold. Had days or months gone by, I wondered. I remembered when I was on the Choctaw Mile the heat was sweltering. How could there be so much snow already. As I glanced up toward the bridge, I saw a man standing there looking at me. How could he see me, I thought. I am a ghost.

I decided the only way I would ever find out was if I went up and tried to talk to him. As I approached, he looked right at me. This is strange. I did not think the living could see the dead but this guy definitely did. Once I reached where he was standing, I said, "Can you see me, mister?"

He said, "Of course I can, Clyde." Now I was really confused so I asked him who he was.

He told me that his name was Clarence. He said, "I am a ghost too, Clyde." I got excited because maybe this man could tell me what to do now. He told me what happened to him and why he was now a ghost. Of course, he was not giving the information I had hoped to hear, like where heaven was and so forth. I just let him ramble on because I figured, sooner or later, he would say something I could use.

As we stood there, Clarence also told me that I would have to use the living to find my answers. I became frustrated with the whole conversation when Clarence spoke up saying, "If you want to know more, my friend, you need to realize that you stayed to complete a task and no one will be able to tell you how to cross to the other side until it is the right time and you are ready."

Why can't I go now? It could be months or years before I knew how to contact a living person. Just as I started to ask him how to do that, I turned to see that he had left me. Aloud I said, "Thanks Clarence. You are a big help."

Time passed in the blink of an eye for me. If I had to guess, years had passed. The cars that I watched travel over the bridge were different, fancier and more brightly colored. A lot of times I wished I had a chance to drive one of them but, obviously, that was never going to happen. I sat there day after day wondering how long it would be before someone would come to this place so I could try to talk to them. It was funny that I had thought that because, the very next day, a car pulled over on the side of the road with what looked to me like a group of teenagers in it. The weather had become nice again so I thought maybe they had come to go swimming in the river. As they made their way down to the water, I followed closely behind them. I did not think it would hurt anything because they could not see me anyway. My intent was not to scare them but to try and talk to them. They threw some blankets down on the ground and the boys ran to jump in the river. Two young ladies sat on the blankets talking about the boys they were with. So how am I going to talk to them, I thought? Then one of the girls said, "Hey, Jane, want to go dive in?"

"No, I don't think so. I don't like to swim," Jane responded. So the first girl ran off to join up with the boys in the water. Jane sat there reading a book so I thought if I am going to do this I better figure out a way soon.

I tried knocking over and moving things on the blanket but she paid the activity no mind. Then I took one end of the blanket and made it fly up. Jane got a strange look on her face and said, "That is strange; there is no wind today." As she looked around, I kicked up some sand so she would notice it. "What in the heck is going on," Jane said? She slowly got to her feet and kept looking all around her. Then I figured if I was ever going to prove that I was there, I would have to give her some kind of final proof of my presence. As she turned to look behind her, I put my hand on her arm, gave it a slight squeeze and let go. I did not want to scare her. Her eyes grew as big as half dollars and she began to scream in terror, running up the hill to the car.

The boys and other girl jumped out of the water ran up the hill to find out what had happened. I felt so bad for what I had done, I ran up the hill to see what they were saying about the experience. As I approached the car, I could see Jane in tears. She was sitting in the back seat as her friends did their best to get answers from her. She told them about all the supernatural activity that she experienced. "I think this place is haunted," Jane said. They all just looked at her like she was crazy and decided it was time to take her home. I really did feel horrible for scaring her that way, but at least now I knew I could get someone's attention. Maybe I should do it easier next time.

Some time had passed when I watched another car pull along the road and stop. This time it was a mother and young girl. From the looks of it, the girl was about the same age as Amanda would be now. At first, I became wary of even trying to communicate with them. The feelings of being near a child again were almost unbearable for me. After all, I thought, that is how

I ended up as a ghost. As I watched the mother and young girl walk by and I looked closer at the girl, a chill ran over me. She had almost the identical looks of Amanda. They could be twins, I thought. Of course she was some years older, maybe 17, but her looks astounded me. How could this be possible? Did she come back somehow? I finally realized it must be a sign that I needed to talk to this girl.

Once they reached the river, mother and daughter both removed their shoes and dipped their feet in the water. I sat down behind them and wondered how to approach them so they would not run off, too. After a few minutes, the girl got up and started to wander off. "Not too far, Gracie," her mother said.

"I won't," she said and continued to walk toward my shack, behind a bush that had grown up. I followed to see where she was going. As she got closer to the shack, I thought that maybe if I just moved the bushes a little bit that would get her attention. I got excited because she did not run when I had moved them before her eyes. It seemed like she had become more curious to take a look. As she pushed back the bushes, she saw the shack and crawled inside. I followed her in to make sure she found my journal. Finally, someone was going to read it.

As she poked around through my belongings, she found my journal under the wooden box where I had put it. She picked it up and spoke out loud what she was reading, "The Journal of Clyde Tucker." She then read the year I had put on the first page. "This has been here for awhile," she said. "It is from 1934." The look on her face was as if her curiosity had now truly been peeked as to who I was. As she began to read the journal, I could see tears well up in her eyes. I wondered what she was reading about that would make her cry so I glanced over her shoulder. She had been reading the part where my parents had died. I suppose it made her sad, thinking of how she would feel if it was her own mother. I guess she must have realized she had been gone for some time and crawled out of the shack with my journal in her hand. She ran back to where her mother was sitting and began chattering on about what she had found. Her mother began to look over the journal saying, "Where did you find this, Gracie?"

"Over there. In a little shack behind those bushes," she said, pointing.

"This is interesting," her mother said. "Let's take this to my office and do some checking on this person, Clyde Tucker."

As they walked back up the hill, I followed. There was no way that I could let them leave without me. I had to know what was going on. I felt such relief at that moment. I climbed into the back seat of their car and sat down. Gosh, I hope I can do this, I thought. I have not ridden in a car since my death. Do ghosts ride in cars? I suppose I will find out, I thought.

As the car rolled forward, I felt no ill effects or strangeness. Finally, the woman drove up in front of an old building that looked like it could have been a library at one time and they got out. I followed them into the building. "Stay here," Gracie's mother told her. "I have to go look for Mr. Watkins." As Gracie and I stood in the hallway waiting for her mother to return, she got a strange look on her face and turned, looking straight at me. Could she see me? "Is someone there?" she asked. Did she know I was there, I wondered? She shrugged and turned back around.

The last thing I wanted to do was scare her when I was so close to achieving my goal. As I looked down the hallway, I could see her mother and a man walking toward us. "Gracie, I would like you to meet my boss, Mr. Watkins."

Gracie smiled and reached out to shake his hand. Mr. Watkins smiled back saying, "Very nice to meet you, Gracie. Now let's go see if we can find out more about this Clyde Tucker and the contents of his journal."

I followed them to a room that had every kind of book, newspaper and photo you could possibly ever look over in a lifetime. I looked around in amazement. Mr. Watkins walked over to a pile of newspapers and said, "Let's start our search here, Janelle. These papers are from 1934; maybe they will give us a clue as to who Mr. Tucker might be."

"Here is something," Janelle said. "An article about a Clyde Tucker being arrested for the murder of a 10 year old girl named Amanda Riley. Oh, my God," she gasped. "We were at the murder site today, Gracie. According to this article, Mr. Tucker, a 24 year old man, was arrested after being found next to Amanda

Riley's body. According to sources, her head had been crushed and she had been raped under the Wicatosh River Bridge in July of 1934."

As I listened to the horrific memories of that night, I thought my fate was set in stone. After reading that, I was sure Janelle would have no reason to look any farther but her reaction was not what I expected. Again she said, "Oh, my God," and began to cry.

"What is wrong, Janelle?" Mr. Watkins asked.

"I knew that girl and her family. I had not heard about this," she responded.

"Who was Amanda Riley, Mom?" Gracie asked.

"There is something I need to tell you," she told Gracie, as tears continued to roll down her cheeks.

"Years ago, Gracie, your father and I tried and tried to have children but it just did not happen. We decided that because there were so many children in dire need of a home, we thought it would be nice to adopt one. One day, when we went to Ashton, we met a couple by the name of Rudy and Evelyn Riley. They were going through some hard times and had very little money. Evelyn had just given birth to twin girls and they were unable to afford to feed them both.

"We talked for some time and told them about wanting to have a child ourselves, but were unable to. After that, we both kind of went our own separate ways. The next day, with fate on our side, we ran into them again. They stopped us on the sidewalk to say, 'We need to ask you folks a question.' Rudy stammered a bit but asked us if we wanted to adopt one of their baby girls. We were quite shocked and elated at the same time. Of course we would, we told them. So, to make a long story short Gracie, you are adopted and you are Amanda's twin sister. After your father was killed in the military, I just did not know how to tell you."

Gracie's mouth dropped open. "So I had a twin that I had no idea about and now I find out that she was murdered. Great timing, Mom," she said, sarcastically.

I was in shock. If I could have fainted, I probably would have. No wonder Gracie looked so familiar. How ironic that both girls were in the same place, one in the past and now one in the present. Amazing, I thought. So now that I know about Gracie and Amanda, how will I ever be able to convince Janelle and Gracie that I did not murder her? As I stood there pondering this, I watched as Mr. Watkins sat there reading my journal.

"Janelle, I have been reading this man's journal wanting to know more about if he had wrote anything about what had happened the day Amanda was killed. Let me read these parts to you and see if you get from it what I did," he said.

He read aloud about the days before the murder when I met those three men and how I did not trust them. He read how I had met up with the families by the bridge and met Rudy, Evelyn and their children. He read about how close I had become with the family, how we had plans to go to Oklahoma City to try to get a job in the factory, and how I had helped around the camp and shared my fish with everyone.

Then he looked up and said, "You need to hear this, Janelle and Gracie." With a serious look on his face, he began to read the part about Eddie Colter and his two friends that had come to the camp on the day Amanda was murdered. He spoke of how I watched them and how Eddie's attention seemed to be on Amanda, watching her play. He also read that Rudy and Eddie had almost come to blows that day over food. "That's where it ends," Mr. Watkins said.

"Something is not right about this man, Clyde Tucker, being arrested for this girl's murder. It just seems too convenient" he said.

"Do you think he was railroaded into this whole thing?" Janelle asked.

"Yes, I do," he said, looking up at her.

Next, they began to pore over more newspapers for more information. Mr. Watkins made a call to his friend, Police Chief Daniels, to see if he could find out more about this case and the chief told him that he would find out what he could.

"Oh, Mr. Watkins, Clyde Tucker was put to death at Choctaw Penitentiary only a week and one half after his arrest," Janelle said.

"What? That is impossible," Mr. Watkins said. "How could they ever get through evidence, a trial and execution in only about a week and one half?"

"It's true," Janelle said.

"This boy was put to death on circumstantial evidence," he said. The phone rang and Mr. Watkins answered. It was Chief Daniels. He told Mr. Watkins that something is wrong with this case. According to the police report from that night they brought him to the jail, the next day he went before Judge Hacker and, without so much as a lawyer, the judge convicted him of the murder and he was immediately transferred to the Choctaw Mile.

He told Mr. Watkins he would contact a prosecuting attorney to see if he could get some type of investigation to get to the bottom of this case.

"John, I know it is too late for this young man, but maybe if he was innocent at least his name would be cleared," the chief said. "This was a travesty of justice like I have never seen before. I am going to make sure everyone involved in this is investigated from the top to the bottom until we find the truth."

Mr. Watkins thanked him and that he could not wait to hear the outcome. After he hung up the phone, he just sat back, shaking his head in disbelief. Janelle began to cry, saying this poor young man and Amanda were both pawns in someone's game.

During the whole exchange, Gracie stood quietly in the corner. She seemed to be in shock. I suppose she could not believe that she had once had a sister, the person accused of murdering her was innocent, and she was adopted. I must say it was nice that there were still people who cared about people like me and wanted to get the truth. I was so happy that Gracie had found my journal. Gracie spoke up telling Janelle that she was going to go for a walk.

For some reason, I felt I needed to go with her. As we walked outside, we made our way to what was a children's playground not far away. She sat down on the end of the slide with her head in her hands. I needed to let her know I was there with her. She had to know that she was not alone. I walked forward so that I was in front of her and made a noise so she could hear me. As she began to raise her head, I used all the energy I had so that I could show myself to her. To be honest, it was kind of comical. It was as if she was taking inventory or something of what she was seeing of me. Finally, she got to my head and I smiled at her. She was a little bit startled but asked who I was.

"Hello, Gracie. My name is Clyde Tucker. I have been with you and your mom all day since you were at the bridge," I said.

"How is this possible?" she asked.

Again I smiled and told her that, somehow, I must have been attached to my journal. "When you picked it up, I was able to go with you. I don't know how long I can stay so you can see me but I wanted you, your mom and Mr. Watkins to know how much I appreciate you believing in my innocence."

"You knew my sister, didn't you?" she asked.

I nodded. "She was a very nice little girl."

"I have seen her in dreams," she said.

I told her that I was a fairly new ghost and did not have all the answers, but I thought that we could visit people from time to time.

"She must have just wanted you to know that she is with you. We have something in common, Gracie. I saw her in a dream the night before I was executed."

"I am so sorry you had to lose your life for something you did not do."

"I suppose it was meant to be this way," I said. "I have to go now, but I will see you again. I promise."

When she got back to the office, Janelle expressed concern.

"I saw him, Mom. I saw Clyde Tucker. He appeared to me at the playground and he told me to tell you and Mr. Watkins thank you for believing his innocence."

I don't think Janelle knew quite what to say about her daughter seeing me, but at least maybe now I can move on. As I waited at the office for the rest of that day to see a bright light or something that would show me the way to heaven, I wondered if it had been too long for me. Would I now have to resign myself to being stuck here for the rest of eternity?

The next morning, shortly after the sun came up, Mr. Watkins showed up at the office. At 8 a.m., the phone rang and I could hear him talking with someone about the journal of Clyde Tucker. I wondered what that was all about so I began to listen intently as to what was being said. As he talked to the person on the phone, he mentioned something about a newspaper article about my journal because, apparently, Judge Hacker and all involved had been arrested for some shady goings on with my case. Also, there was a mention about Eddie Colter and how he had been arrested for the murder of Amanda Riley.

Finally, I thought. He had been caught for armed robbery and now, with the journal to give substance to his guilt, he was sitting his butt on death row at the Choctaw Mile just like I had done so many years before. Finally, after all these years, the injustice of my execution and Amanda's death was now over. What a relief, I thought.

Just as I began to wonder how I was going to leave, I turned to see my parents and Amanda standing there in the doorway looking and smiling at me.

"It is time for you to come home now, son," my dad said. Amanda stepped forward, putting her hand on my arm and said, "Now you know the truth about us and how you had became so important to me and my sister's life. Thank you, Clyde. Now let's go. It is time."

So, with a smile on my face, I was going home, leaving behind the nightmare I had lived for so long.

THE END

Faith No More

Written By: Daniel Norvell

Chapter One

Faith no more

How was I going to find this kid when I have been dead for more than 50 years? The world has changed so much in that time. I have observed the senseless acts of many in the time since I took my last breath on this Earth. I have just seven short days, to find a boy and make him aware that he is more than what he realizes.

The world is such an unfriendly place. I cannot think of a worse time to need humanity to be faithful. I was given seven days and only five were left. I'm not sure where I am. I know I am in the United States, in the Midwest. Not much else is clear to me. The boy resides in this city and I have to find him. I cannot fail.

If I fail, humanity ends. If humanity ends, it means that it was a mistake. I remember the Archangel Michael saying to me, "Father, you have been chosen. You have been chosen for your faith. If humanity is proven to be a mistake, Heaven and Earth will crumble. Never forget what is at stake, Father. Never forget that eternity hangs on the soul of this one boy."

There was a lot riding on my shoulders. I have never lost faith, but my faith has always been in the Lord. Now, I need to have faith in myself. I often think that maybe Michael should have picked another candidate.

I was sitting in a Catholic church, praying that I can find this boy. It was around midday and the church had only two other people in it. They were near the front of the church, praying. The door in the back opened and closed. A boy walked in and lay down on the pew next to me. He looked tired. He looked like he hasn't eaten in days. The door opened once more, the boy curled up tight and there he stayed, very still.

Two boys walked in, one with a gun in hand. They looked around and left. The boy, still lying there, asked "Are they gone, Father?"

"They are," I replied. "What is your name, son?"

"My name is Peter. I don't know my last name, Father. I never had one. They don't assign last names at the orphanage."

"Why were those boys chasing you, Peter?" I asked.

"They were going to kill a puppy in the alley over on Jackson Street. I shoved the one with the gun and the puppy ran. They chased me and shot once. I know the bullet came close. I could hear it whiz by my ear."

I placed my hand on Peter's arm and said, "Son, you rest. I will be sitting right here when you wake."

The exhausted boy fell asleep within minutes. I knew I had found the boy I sought.

Chapter Two

The Story of Good Vs. Evil

Peter slept for hours. As promised, I didn't leave his side. He finally stirred and asked, "Father, why do bad things have to happen?"

"Son, bad things happen to everyone, everyday. The Lord never gives you more than you can deal with. Always keep in mind, Peter, that if everything in the world was good all of the time, many people would have nothing to look forward to and no reason for faith. The bad is sometimes what makes us cherish those good times even more."

Peter smiled. "I guess you're right, Father."

He proceeded to tell me that he only had blurred visions of his parents. He could not remember the last time he had seen them and that, one day, they were just gone. The orphanage was not a nice place. H lifted his shirt to show me the scars across his back.

"Father, do you think that losing my parents could have been wrong? Do you think that maybe it should have happened to someone else instead of me?"

"Let me tell you a story, son. It is a story that has been told many times, in many ways. This is my gift to you because I have never shared it with anyone."

I told Peter of a time when Heaven and Earth were closer than they are now. I told him of an angel so beautiful and wise that the Lord cherished him. The Lord has no favorites, but the Lord really felt that this angel was more than the rest. It made the Lord proud, but it also made Him uneasy at the same time. Pride can be good, but it can also be bad. The Lord created man. Mankind cherished the Lord and the Lord loved them.

Over time, mankind began to show the pride that the angel did. The angel had been coming to Earth and placing false ideas into the mind of mankind. The Lord called on the angel and asked him why. The angel replied that he could be a better creator than the Lord. The Lord cast him out of Heaven and gave him his own realm to rule and create in. That realm is Hell.

Before his departure, the angel told the Lord that mankind was a mistake. If the angel were to ever prove this, Heaven and Earth would collide and crumble; all existence as we know it would no longer be. The Lord had a safeguard in place—he could wipe out humanity, such as he did with a great flood, and cleanse the Earth of mankind. If mankind no longer exists, there is no mistake.

The angel, so twisted by his own pride and envy of our Lord, promised that he would never stop trying to make the Lord realize his mistake.b It is better for the angel, who is really now the creator of the realm of demons, to bide his time and let his twisted beliefs bleed through into our world and ultimately try to prove that the Lord is wrong. If that ever were to happen, we would all be wiped from the slate of creation.

Peter stared at me in awe. He finally spoke. "Father? Do you think it is possible? Do you think that the angel will be able to prove that mankind was a mistake?"

"Son, every day Mothers kill their babies, children are killing children. Sin is all about us, everywhere," I replied. "It is being committed without repent. I think, Peter, that if mankind were ever to be proven to be a mistake . . . here and now would be the chance that the angel needs.

"Mankind has one chance. It can be saved by one soul. That soul has to realize that he is more than what he appears. His worth may not appear to be much here but the very fabric of existence hangs on him. I only hope that he realizes it in time."

Peter shuddered. "I hope he does, Father. I hope he does." Peter lay back down; the poor boy hadn't slept in days. "Father, do you care if I sleep some more here? It's the only place I feel safe; the only place that is calm."

"Rest for the night, child. I will remain at your side for as long as you need me to," I responded.

Peter fell asleep with a smile on his face. I placed my hand on his head and prayed. I prayed this boy would realize that he was the key to existence. The fate of humanity, the fate of creation, rested on his shoulders. As Peter slept, one day melted into the next; one day closer to the end.

Chapter Three

Answers Lead To More Questions

Peter slept for the rest of the night and most of the morning. He finally woke up and told me he was hungry. I hadn't felt hunger in many years so I told Peter to walk over to the basket by the door and take out enough money for breakfast. It was my feeling that it was more important for the church to feed this hungry boy than anything else those few dollars might be used for.

We walked a few blocks to a small diner and sat in a booth. I could smell the coffee; I missed the taste of coffee. Peter placed his order and asked if I would like some coffee. The waitress stared at Peter as if he were crazy. I raised my hand and shook my head no.

As Peter ate, he described to me the final days he had spent with his parents and little sister. He said that he missed all of them very much and was unclear of the events that had taken them from him. Peter told me that he was riding his new bicycle that his parents had just given him for his birthday and that he was riding very fast. Peter was not sure how but he was thrown from the bike, hit his head, and was knocked out. Peter said he woke up to no bike and walked home. When Peter arrived home, his parents and sister were gone. I found his story very odd but I did not question him about it. I had seen his scars; someone had taken him to that orphanage and Peter may have blocked it from his mind.

Peter paid the waitress and we left the diner. We spent the day walking and talking and I was not sure when we were going to be made aware of any event on the horizon. We walked by a park and Peter stopped in his tracks. "What's wrong, son?" I asked.

"That's the park where the voices are, Father. The voices call to me every time I pass this park; they call to me to come in to the light. The light took my parents and my little sister. I stay away because I don't want it to take me, too." The boy's voice trembled. Clearly, he was terrified of this park or whatever was in it that created the chatter that Peter was hearing.

"I think they are ghosts, Father."

This was a difficult situation for me to discuss with Peter since I'm a ghost. To this boy, I was as real as he is. "Son, they may or may not be ghosts but have faith that the Lord will not let them harm you. Your faith will see you through the darkest of times."

We walked for a few more hours and I found something very odd. The city was very loud but, as we walked, we didn't pass anyone. I had not seen a single car drive by, yet I could hear traffic all around. Dusk was coming and Peter asked if we could return to the church because he said he felt cold.

We made our way back to the church and I could swear that the church was on the opposite corner of the intersection than when we left this morning. We entered the church. The benches were a different color and the candles were in different places. Something is very wrong here, I thought to myself. The same two people, a man and a woman, still prayed. They faced toward the alter and paid no attention to Peter. In all of my years as a priest, this was the first time I had ever felt uneasy in a church. Something was not right and I now lost another day looking for the answers I needed to help this boy save humanity.

Chapter Four

The Trip To The Park

Peter slept restlessly that night. I knew we needed to return to the park for answers. Peter jerked awake. "Father! Father!"

"Yes? I am here, son."

Peter appeared very upset and confused. "Father, I can hear my sister and parents calling my name. They were calling to me all night long, like I was dreaming it."

I told the boy that I was not sure what it could mean, but I assured him that I would stay with him as long as I could. I asked Peter if he was hungry and he said he wasn't. He told me that, even when he eats, his stomach still feels empty. There were so many things going on that I could not explain and this was another one. I had watched that boy eat like a horse and now it made sense why he ate so much.

I was running out of time; I needed to get to that park. It was the park that held the key. It's where the battle will begin. Peter and I needed to go there to stop whatever was coming. I spent the next three hours trying to convince Peter to return to the park with me. He finally agreed under one condition: I had to promise I would stay by his side and not leave him.

"Son, I will not leave your side if I don't have to. Know this here and now—you are by far one of the bravest boys I have ever met and someday you will change the world. That much I can assure you."

We set out for the park. The day was hot and there was a strange odor in the air. It smelled of a hospital. I recognized the smell from all of the times I had visited hospitals to administer the Last Rights to the dead and dying.

Peter and I walked in silence. I had more questions than answers. What is this boy to do? Has he not suffered enough? What could be in this park to bring about the end of all creation?

We arrived at the park and I found it odd that it seemed farther from the church than it did yesterday. Peter was clearly apprehensive.

"Don't you hear them, Father? Don't you hear the voices calling to me? They are calling my name!"

I heard nothing but the wind gently rustling the trees. "What are the voices saying, son?"

"They are asking me to come to the light, to come home."

I wasn't sure what it all meant but we continued on into the park. Peter seemed even more melancholy. "Father, the voices want me to come into the light but all I can see is a darkened park!"

"Let's keep walking, son. Maybe something will come to us."

We walked for what seemed to be hours and, suddenly, we were at the front gates of the park where we had entered. "Peter, we have walked in a straight line ever since we entered this park, have we not?"

"Yes, Father, we have. Why are we back at the front gates?"

I didn't have an answer for him. "Let's return to the church, Peter. Night is coming and I am not sure we should be out in it when it arrives."

Peter clutched my sleeve. "Father, we won't have very far to go." The church was now across the street from the park. I just stood there, awestruck. There was not a church there before, let alone the very church where we spent the last two nights.

"What does it mean, Father?"

"I don't know, son, but whatever it means, we need to get inside."

There were two reasons we needed to get into the church. The first was that night was coming. The second was that I could hear the voices calling to the boy.

Chapter Five

Voices Keep Calling

The voices called to Peter all night long. I could hear them, too. It was strange that it seemed to be three different voices calling. I couldn't make out what they were saying but I think Peter could. He sat in a corner of the church, his arms clasped around his knees.

"Father, maybe I should go to the light. Maybe it is meant to be," he said finally. I was not sure what to say. If this boy dies, we all cease to exist according to St. Michael.

"Peter, you will know what to do when the time comes." That was the only advice I had to offer.

Later that night, the entire church began to shake as if in an earthquake. I rushed to the boy's side. "Peter, whatever happens . . . I will always be with you, son."

Peter smiled at me. "You were sent from heaven, Father. I know because you are the first person since the accident that has ever spoken to me."

"I was Peter and I will be here as long as heaven allows me to remain with you."

The church began to fall apart. "Peter, run outside. I'll be right behind you!"

We ran out of the church and it seemed that all of creation was crumbling. The only thing that stood out to us was the light showing through the park. I heard the voices clearly now.

"Peter, wake up. We are all here waiting."

I heard a voice that I hadn't heard before say, "It's time, folks. You can stay with him after I shut the machines off. I'll return after he is gone."

I immediately knew what was happening. "Peter! Run, son! Run as fast as you can to that light!"

"I am scared, Father!"

"Don't be afraid! I will always be with you! Always!"

Peter ran for the light as fast as he could. The park, the church and everything collapsed around me. Then it was quiet. I was standing in a hospital room with a man, a woman and a little girl. Lying in the bed was a boy. He had tubes everywhere and I could barely recognize him. He opened his eyes. I knew it was Peter the instant I saw his blue eyes.

The woman ran from the room, "Doctor! Doctor! DOCTOR!"

It finally made sense. Peter had awakened from his sleep, a sleep that must have been protecting his mind from an accident. Peter looked directly at me. I winked at him and I was gone. I returned to St. Michael and asked him what happened.

"The decision had to be the boy's to make. He had to decide to go into the light before the family decided to pull the life support that sustained him. The boy had created an entire world. It protected his mind while his body healed. He will be fine, Father."

Everything the boy had told me was the truth as he perceived it. Years later, I would be called by St. Michael again to make one more trip involving Peter. It had been almost 20 years since I had seen the boy. St. Michael advised me that this is why Peter had to live. This act that I would witness would be Peter's contribution to humanity, his contribution to the world. It would not have been possible if I had not been there to tell Peter to walk into the light. I asked St. Michael when I would be leaving. "Soon, Father. Very soon," he said.

Chapter Six

Peter's Gift

It was fall, although I don't know the year. For the second time since my death, I am being sent to help the same boy. St. Michael told me I was going to witness an event and Peter would need me.

"It's time for you to go back, Father."

"I am ready."

The next thing I knew, I was standing in a house watching a man shave. He looked into the mirror and I looked at the reflection. Those eyes gave him away in an instant: it was Peter. He put on his shirt, slung his gun holster over his shoulder and then put on his coat. Peter had become a police officer. I followed him into the living room.

"Hello, son," I said, but he couldn't hear or see me. I thought it best that I follow Peter and see if I could figure out what I needed to do for him. Peter worked for the Secret Service in the nation's capitol. He was assigned to the high priority division that protects diplomatic visitors to America. I heard Peter's superior tell him he was to protect the Pope tonight at a speech.

This Pope had been instrumental in trying to negotiate peace in some pretty nasty spots in the world, according to the briefing Peter was hearing. There are many people who would like to see him harmed.

Peter spent most of his day doing paperwork and studying the set up for his assignment. He would be the agent closest to the Pope. The other guys teased him on the way out of the office that day. "See you in the pressure cooker tonight, Pete."

"See you tonight, guys," he responded with a smile.

Peter went home to gather his things and relax. Before he left, he got a phone call from his mother. "Say hello to the Pope for me and be careful, son."

"I always am, Mom. Goodnight."

Peter went to his closet and pulled out a small box. He removed a crucifix and placed it around his neck. He put on his bulletproof vest and his gun. "Father, if you are still with me, if you are still watching, please watch over my team tonight."

"I will, son." I could tell that Peter was apprehensive about his assignment. He was very nervous about something. Anytime you have a Pope visit, it has to be a dangerous event for all involved.

It was time to start the banquet. The team was briefing and Peter's superior said, "Pete, I am sticking you at point. I need my best man closest to the Pope." Peter nodded.

The Pope arrived and started to speak. The crowd was enormous. As the Pope spoke, a man stood up and reached into his jacket. Peter started to reach into his jacket as well but the man pulled out a napkin to blow his nose. I could see Peter shake his head and continue to scan the crowd.

Dinner was being served and waiters moved among the tables. The Holy Father continued his speech and the crowd listened while they ate. I remembered the first time I had seen a Pope speak years ago. I knelt and said a prayer for this Pope and for the people there. I asked the Lord to especially look out for Peter and his team tonight. As I finished praying, the wait staff started to serve desert.

I thought to myself, a little bit longer and Peter is finished with his assignment. Maybe Michael sent me here to watch over Peter. The waiter picking up trays at the table directly in front of the Pope spun around. "Gun!" is all I heard before two shots rang out. After the second shot was fired, I saw the waiter slump to the ground. There was a lot of commotion and the Holy Father was rushed from the building in about 10 seconds flat.

I made my way to the front of the room. What I saw made me sick. Peter lay on the floor in front of where the Pope had been speaking. He was shot in the throat and one of the officers with him was holding pressure on it.

"Stay with me, Pete. Stay with me!" I could see Peter drifting in and out of consciousness and his blue eyes fixed on me. He tried to speak but nothing came out. I knelt beside him as his eyes were fixed on mine. He tried to say "Father . . ."

"Peter, I am here, son. I am here to bring you home."

Peter gasped and his eyes began to roll back into his head. The paramedics arrived, loaded Peter into the ambulance and raced to the hospital. The doctors worked for two hours to try to save Peter. I waited.

I was sitting outside Peter's room when a boy walked up to me and said, "Father? Is there someone here for you to see?"

I asked the boy, who I had never seen before, "Son, you can see me?"

"Of course, Father. All of us here can see you."

I looked up and I was no longer in the hospital. I was standing in a room filled with children. "Where am I?" I asked.

"You were about to say the opening prayer for our breakfast, Father. Are you OK?"

Was I dreaming? I was back in my church and it was the morning of my death. I wondered why Michael was letting me see this. I shook my head and turned around to lead the prayer but the church was empty. I was standing in a funeral home and a priest was talking with Peter's parents and sister and her children. I moved closer to the conversation.

"I was just a boy when Father O'Brien died," the priest said. "I was the last one to speak with him that morning. I asked him if he was Ok and he had the stroke. He died before he hit the ground. I remember his gentle face and his reassuring eyes, but Father O'Brien was dead for years before your son was born."

Peter's mother spoke. "Peter had an accident when he was younger. While he was in a coma, he said that a priest helped him find our voices in the light. The reason I am asking is that when Peter died, he kept mouthing 'Father, Father take me with you.'"

The priest shook his head, "It defies explanation. I know if I were to have a guardian angel, Father O'Brien would be the one I'd choose."

The priest gave a sermon later at the church and called Peter a hero. He explained that not only did Peter serve his country, but he also served the Lord by saving the Holy Father. The priest then read a note written by the Pope himself, commending Peter and his bravery and extending his condolences to Peter's family.

I followed the procession to the cemetery and watched as they laid Peter to rest. I stood there for a long time after the people had gone. I said a prayer and looked toward the sky. "Michael? What am I supposed to do? This boy gave his life and I am still not sure what the mission is."

I heard a voice behind me. "Father? Thank you for coming. I always knew you would be the one that the Lord would send for me should I ever pass in the line of duty." It was Peter.

"I wish I hadn't seen you again in this way, son. It was an honorable thing you did for the Holy Father; the reason you needed to survive when you were a boy."

"I know, Father. I have never forgotten you. I saw you there at my side after the shooting and I saw you at the hospital. I am ready to go with you now, Father."

Peter and I set out across the cemetery and into the light of heaven.

A year later, the Pope helped the countries of the world disarm their nuclear arsenals. If Peter had not saved the Holy Father, it never would have happened. He saved humanity and he had faith to know that God would send me for him when he took that bullet. Heaven and Earth would not crumble because this boy proved that it is not a mistake.

There were still people in the world that held faith in humanity. The faith of one man did save creation. The fallen angel would have to wait another few thousand years when humanity again began to forget the Lord that put them here. The actions of one person saved all of creation.

The sad thing to me was that nobody on Earth will ever be aware of the true hero that Peter was. Peter did what Jesus did: he died for all of their sins.

THE END

The Widow Walk

Written By: Sandy Wells

Chapter One

My Happiest Day

As we walked up the path along the cliff toward the lighthouse which was to be our new home, I could hear the crashing of the waves below us. The smell of the sea was an amazing experience that most people would never have the opportunity to enjoy. I was truly blessed. I felt almost honored to be joining my new husband, Charles, to tend this wonderful lighthouse with him. He had made his life within its sturdy walls for some time now. We had met many months before in the port town of Dalsmith where my parents resided and ran their fishing supply business along the docks.

As I grew into a young woman, it was often up to me to care for the business for my parents. I had many men in our port town interested in calling on me, but none caught my eye more than Charles Dowdy with his sturdy build and handsome features. Until his decision to become the lighthouse keeper, he had been a seaman traveling the great oceans and trading in all the great ports of the world. He often spoke of how the sea still called to him as if it was a woman whispering in his ear to come home. However, once we met, he told me that his life at sea was over. He wanted to stay with me in Dalsmith and raise a proper family. That is how I ended up walking this path toward that grand lighthouse. Attached to the lighthouse was a beautiful home of Victorian style with astonishing architecture. Charles had already brought me here many times but this day was the most special of all because it was now mine to cherish for the rest of my life.

As we arrived at the lighthouse and our new home together, Charles swept me into his arms and carried me across the threshold. I knew at that moment that I could never be happier.

We spent the next few hours sitting together, staring out the front window and watching the sea. He told me of great sea tales and his adventures. Finally, the time came for him to tend the lighthouse so off he went to leave me to my wifely duties preparing food for his meals that day and cleaning. It was wonderful to know that I finally had a home of my own and a husband that I truly adored.

That evening, after the day's duties were complete, Charles came in the front door to my waiting arms and a table full of delicious foods. Being accustomed to helping my mother prepare food for a large family, I made too much for the two of us to consume.

"My dear Gwyneth, are you trying to make me into a round, pot-bellied man?" he asked, giggling.

"No, my sweet husband," I replied, looking around the table, realizing just how much food I had laid out. We both chuckled at such a sight.

After stuffing ourselves, we went to the living area to enjoy the rest of the evening together. I wanted to do some reading so I sat in the chair next to the fireplace. Charles sat in the chair across from me, smoking his pipe and gazing into the fire as its flames danced upwards from the coals. I looked up from my reading to see him staring at me.

"What are you looking at, Charles?" I asked.

He looked me in the eyes and said, "I am looking at such a radiant creature that I can not take my eyes off of her."

I smiled and told him how silly he was being. Some time later, Charles said it was time for bed because the next day would be an early one. I agreed and we climbed the stairs to the second floor where our bedroom was located. After all, this was our first night together as husband and wife. To be honest, I was quite tired but I did not want to disappoint my new husband.

As the sun came up the next morning, I turned to find Charles already up and leaving to tend the lighthouse for the day.

"So early, my dear?" I asked.

He turned to me and replied, "Yes, my dear Gwyneth, but please do not get up yet. The day will have to wait a little bit longer before it sees your beautiful face."

So, as he requested, I turned back over and fell directly back to sleep. I slept for some time before waking to a gorgeous, sunny day. How could things ever get any better, I wondered? I proceeded down the stairs in my night dress to make a proper breakfast for Charles. About an hour later, Charles entered through the front door saying, "Good morning, sleepyhead." I laughed and continued setting the table.

As I looked up from my plate, I could see him pondering over a paper in his hand. "What do you have there, my dear?" I asked.

He began to tell me about a sea captain coming into port today that owed him money and he was going into town later to meet up with him. I asked if I might go with him to get some supplies and he agreed it would be a good idea.

Charles also said that, because of the treacherous path we had to take to get to town, he would appreciate if I would never travel it alone. I promised I would not and went off to get ready for our journey into Dalsmith. As we arrived in town, Charles left me to go wait for the ship's captain while I went to do my shopping. Since I was in town, I stopped by my parents' shop to tell them about my new home and how wonderful I felt being married. My parents were quite happy for me. It seemed like we had been in town for some time, and I knew that the lighthouse was not going to tend itself, so I excused myself and went to search for Charles.

As I walked along the docks, I could see what looked like a clipper ship. I thought that must be the ship that Charles had been waiting for so I made my way through the bustle of people working on the docks. As I arrived at the ship, I saw Charles and an older gentleman standing on the deck speaking to each other. I saw a crew member preparing to board the ship and asked him if I could come aboard. I pointed to Charles, telling him he is my husband. "Of course, ma'am. You are welcome to come aboard," he said.

"Oh, hello, my dear Gwyneth," Charles said as I approached. And he introduced me to Captain Winston.

"Nice to meet you, Gwyneth. Charles was just telling me about his beautiful new bride. He was absolutely correct. You are breathtaking," Captain Winston said.

To be honest, he rather embarrassed me. I could feel my face blushing. "It is very nice to meet you as well, Captain Winston."

We stood there making small talk for a short time, but then I touched Charles' arm and reminded him that the lighthouse would need tending soon.

Charles just chuckled and said, "Yes, you are correct, my dear. I am afraid we must be on our way, Captain," and we said our goodbyes.

As we reached the bottom of the gangplank, the captain yelled out to Charles. "Don't forget what we talked about, my friend." Charles waved and said that he wouldn't.

"I don't mean to be a curious wife but what did you talk about?" I asked. Charles said we could talk about it over dinner. I agreed and we made our way back to the lighthouse. As we walked up the narrow path toward the lighthouse, Charles seemed distracted so I asked if he was alright. He smiled and assured me he was.

Finally, we reached the lighthouse. It was quite dark when we both noticed that the beacon on the lighthouse seemed very dim. Since this lighthouse was how the ships made their way through this treacherous passage, Charles ran the rest of the way so he could see what happened. As I entered the lighthouse, I saw Charles making a mad dash up the stairs with a can of kerosene.

"The light has gone out and I know that two ships are making way out of the port tonight. I have to hurry," he told me, breathlessly.

As Charles worked on the beacon light, I walked outside to see the fog rolling in over the bay. I thought maybe I should start blowing the fog horn in case there might already be a ship out there in the fog. The horn was so loud, it nearly deafened me. But, I thought, at least if they could hear the horn, they would be able to tell if they were near the cliffs and turbulent waters.

After relighting the beacon, Charles came down to the house. I figured he would be hungry so I hurriedly began preparing a hot meal for him. After we ate, Charles said he needed to talk with me about something.

"You look so serious. Is everything alright?" I asked.

"I have the opportunity to go with Captain Winston out to sea for a short time and I need to know what you feel about that."

I looked directly into his big brown eyes and said, "My dear Charles, if that is what you want to do then I suppose I will support you. How long would you be gone?"

"It might take up to three months, my dear."

"Oh my goodness," I gasped, and lowered my head so he couldn't see the sadness in my eyes.

"Don't be sad," he said. "Captain Winston told me that he would not have asked at all, but he must get this last shipment into the port up the east coast before the fall storms hit."

I was not happy and I could not tell Charles not to go, but I was concerned about who was going to tend the lighthouse. I knew I would not be able to manage on my own.

"I have made arrangements with a couple of men in town to help you with the lighthouse maintenance and also to watch over you while I am gone," he said.

"When will you be leaving?" I asked.

He said he was leaving in the morning and reassured me he wouldn't leave without waking me. After he drifted off, I quietly cried myself to sleep at the thought of how much I was going to miss my new husband.

Chapter Two

Joy and Loss

The next morning came too quickly. Charles was sitting next to me on the bed saying, "I believe I am ready to go."

"Must you go?" I asked.

"I have already given Captain Winston my word that I would be with him on this voyage. He wants skilled sailing mates because of the dangers of the area we have to sail into."

I just looked at him and sighed. "I understand how you are feeling," he said.

"I will be fine," I said, "but my concern is not for me."

"No need to worry about me. I am a skilled seaman, my dear."

"I know, but that does not make this any easier." He smiled and embraced me in his loving arms. "Hurry home, my love," I said as he rose and walked out the door.

I did not want to miss him sailing by the lighthouse so I climbed out of bed to dress quickly. As I sat in the chair by the window with a perfect view of the channel below, I had the most horrible feeling that I was never going to see him again.

As I sat there waiting for daylight to come, I heard a knock on front door and went to answer it. At the door was George Williams, a good friend of my parents and of Charles, as well. At least it was not a stranger, I thought.

"Good morning, Gwyneth. I am here to tend the lighthouse as I told Charles I would," he said. He told me that if I needed anything, not to hesitate to ask. I thanked him and he went to the lighthouse. As he walked away, I called to him and said that breakfast would be ready shortly and that if he would like to stay in the room in the lighthouse while Charles was gone, he was more than welcome.

He was an elderly gentleman and I trusted him completely to do the job. George had lost his wife several years before so I knew it really was not necessary that he make that long walk back and forth into town. I told him to make himself a bed in the lighthouse. Well, at least that is one less worry that I will have while Charles is gone, I thought. George is very dependable.

As the sun rose, I scurried up the stairs to the widow walk on top of the house where Charles would be able to see me and I could wave to him. As I stood there, I saw the ship coming closer and I could see Charles on deck next to the captain's wheel waving frantically at me. I began to wave, too. As I watched the ship grow smaller, I could not shake the bad feeling in my heart. I knew that Captain Winston was an excellent seaman and would take every precaution necessary, but it did not help. I knew I had household duties as well as those I could help George with in the lighthouse. I hoped they would keep me occupied so time would pass quickly.

Days ran together and, before I knew it, a month-and-a-half had passed with my daily visits to the widow walk to look for the white sails of Captain Winston's ship on the horizon. Everything ran smoothly with George to help me. I knew if Charles had been correct about the time frame in which he would return, it was now only a few weeks away. My heart jumped for joy at the thought of having my love back home.

One fine day, after finishing my chores, I decided that supplies were getting somewhat shy so I walked out to the lighthouse to ask George to accompany me to town. Even though Charles was not there, I remembered what he said about walking the narrow path on the cliff so I wanted to respect his wishes.

Once in town, I went directly to my parents' shop to talk to them. The weeks that had passed were lonely and I needed to see a familiar face.

"You look pale, Gwyneth. Are you taking care of yourself since Charles left?" my mother asked.

"Of course, Mother. I am just not sleeping well. I am very anxious for Charles to return," I responded.

"You might want to go see the doctor while you are in town," she said.

"I am fine but if you insist, I will go see him right now." I knew that if I did not go, my mother would hound me until I did. The doctor's office was in his home so I walked up and knocked on the door. His cleaning lady came to the door and invited me in to wait for the doctor to return from a house call.

The door opened and Dr. Stone entered and said, "Hello, Gwyneth. How is married life treating you, young lady?"

I just smiled and he told me to follow him into his office. After he examined, me he asked when Charles was supposed to be back.

"Hopefully in a few weeks," I said.

"That is really good because I have some news for you, Gwyneth."

I looked at him, thinking I must have something terribly wrong with me.

He smiled and said, "You are with child, my dear."

"You must be mistaken, doctor," I said.

"No. I guarantee in about seven months, you will be a mother," he said, still smiling.

After the initial shock wore off, I was ecstatic. I am going to be a mother! Charles will be so pleased.

As I walked back to my parents' shop, I was in a daze.

The first words out of my mother's mouth were, "What did the doctor say?"

With a big smile, I told her my big news. She and my father both cheered with delight at the thought of being grandparents. After spending a little more time talking with them, I told them I had to get back home.

"Have you seen George?" I asked my father.

"Yes. He told me that he would meet you at the Anderson's Mercantile," my father said.

I said goodbye to my parents and went to meet George. I felt a little sad that Charles wasn't the first person I told about our child, but I knew he would understand how excited I was about this glorious news. Anderson's Mercantile was a few blocks away so I walked slowly, meeting up with locals I knew and sharing my happy news. As I reached the mercantile, I could see George waiting patiently on the bench in front of the store. I had to tell George about my condition. He said that under no circumstances would Charles allow me to venture back into town in my delicate condition.

"I will do the trading from now on until Charles arrives home," George said.

I agreed and we went in the mercantile, gathered the supplies I needed and turned back toward home.

The next morning was a beautiful sunny day with the world seeming more amazing than I could ever remember. The thought of having my own child to pamper and adore was still too wonderful to imagine. I made my way to the widow walk for my daily watch of the horizon I saw what looked like a ship. I was so excited that I made my way quickly down the stairs, through my bedroom and down to the main floor to gather my coat so I could stand by the lighthouse for a better look. Then I noticed it was not the ship I was hoping to see. I became rather depressed but then thought well maybe tomorrow and went back into the house.

As the day passed, I watched a large bank of dark black clouds gather in the horizon. Just about that time, George knocked on the door and entered. He told me that a severe storm was heading our way so he would be staying close to the light for the rest of the night to keep it shining bright. I thanked him and asked if he would secure the shutters so they would not bang around in the wind. He agreed and went to get things in order for the coming storm.

As I watched the storm rage outside, I asked God to keep Charles safe. Sometime during the early morning hours after the storm had passed, a man came to deliver a message to George.

The message read, "The Emma T has been lost. The ship was dashed into the cliff, broke apart and all aboard perished," according to a chief dock man in the small coastal town of Leandar."

Sadly, George wondered how he would tell me.

Chapter Three

Where is Charles?

As I began to stir, a feeling that something was wrong came over me. I slowly sat up on the edge of my bed trying to shake the horrible feeling of emptiness. Maybe this is part of how a woman feels when she is with child, I thought. So I shrugged my shoulders and began to dress for the day ahead. The next thing I knew, a knock came on the front door and I hurried downstairs to answer it. When I opened the door, I saw George just standing there with his head hung low. He glanced up to look me in the eye.

"My dear Gwyneth, I have some bad news." He did not have to say anything more. I knew Charles had died aboard that ship. George read me the message he had received. As I stood there staring at George, I felt my body go cold and everything went black.

I suppose I must have fainted because when I opened my eyes, my mother was sitting in the chair next to the bed.

"Oh Mother, please tell me that I just had a horrible dream and my Charles will be coming home soon," I pleaded.

With tears in her eyes she said, "My dear, sweet child, he is never coming home again."

I wailed in torment of the loss of my only true love. I wept for our child that Charles would never get to meet.

"You must stop this, dear. You will make yourself sick," my mother advised.

"I don't care, Mother. How will I ever be able to survive without him? Will my child ever truly know who his father was?"

My mother sat with me for days as I wept uncontrollably, urging me to eat and keep my health strong for my child. Horrible thoughts passed through my mind. I lashed out in anger, blaming everyone for what had happened when it was fate alone that took Charles from me.

Every day that passed, I felt weaker and weaker. Dr. Stone came to visit me on several occasions at the request of my family. The look on his face spoke his concern for my well being.

After a few days, I finally found the will to get out of my bed. I cannot describe how I felt. It was almost as if I was standing outside of myself and the person in the mirror was someone I did not know. Strange thoughts passed through my mind and I found myself making daily trips to the widow walk to watch for that ship that would never return. It became difficult to distinguish between my thoughts and this person I saw myself turning into.

One day, as my mother went to draw me a bath, I sat in the chair by the window, the same spot I had watched Charles leave me so long ago. I no longer had any desire for life; it had all faded. My hopes and dreams for a life with the man I cherished were gone. Suddenly, my stomach began to cramp severely and I slid to the floor with a crash. I hear my mother yelling my name.

"Gwyneth! Gwyneth are you alright, my child?"

"Help me, Mother," I cried out. As I looked down I could see a large spot of blood on my night dress. I curled into a ball to try to ease the pain. George had been downstairs speaking with my mother and ran up after her to help. As they entered the room, they saw me lying on the floor writhing in pain. George picked me up and laid me on my bed.

"My baby. Oh God, please, do not let me lose my child. It is all I have left of Charles," I prayed, silently.

George told my mother that he would run to get Dr. Stone and out the door he went. My mother sat on the side of my bed, stroking my hair and softly whispering to me. I lay there in extreme pain for what seemed like forever, slipping in and out of consciousness. I could hear my mother praying quietly. Suddenly, I felt very strange and I could not breathe well. I opened my eyes slightly, looked around the room, saw my mother looking down at me and then that was all.

As I awoke from that horrible dream, I was standing next to the window. Dr. Stone, my mother and George were all gathered around the bed. As I glanced down, I saw what looked like someone lying on the bed. As I walked to the end of the bed, I saw that my mother was in tears and Dr. Stone was comforting her.

The doctor explained that because of my weakened state, I miscarried and began to hemorrhage. Nothing could have been done, he said.

"They are talking about me," I thought. My body lay on the bed. How is this possible? If I am dead, how am I standing here? Then thoughts of Charles raced through my head. I once had read about a man that believed that after we die, our souls go to heaven and sometimes they stayed in a form that he called a ghost or apparition of our soul.

I felt wonderful and full of life. I don't want to be dead. What about my baby? If there is someplace called heaven then where was it and how do I get there? What about Charles? Why was he not here as a ghost with me. It seemed like he would want to be with me now. My mind whirled with questions, but no answers came to me. I sat down in my chair by the window gazing out at the sparkling sea. It was my favorite thing to do when I was waiting for Charles to come back. What was going to happen now? I am not sure how long I had sat in that chair staring out the window, but I began to hear a strange noise that sounded vaguely familiar, as if the shutters on the windows were being closed. What in the world was going on?

As I turned my attention back to the window, I saw George sticking himself halfway out of my bedroom window closing them. How am I going to be able to see if they are closed, I thought? This was very strange that he could not see me sitting there. I suppose that is the way of it; living people could not see those who have died. Very odd, I thought.

As he began to walk away toward my bedroom door, I wondered if there was some way to let him know that I was there. I reached up and unclasped the latch on the shutter.

The wind must have caught it because it flew open and hit with a bang. It hit so hard and made such an atrocious noise that George was startled and almost ran from the room before stopping in his tracks and turning to see the shutters wide open.

I am guessing he thought it was strange, but walked back over to relock them.

"That is interesting. How did that happen?" he said aloud. I giggled to myself. This was going to be fun, I thought. It was like playing a childhood game. Yet I still wondered why I did not see Charles. I had so many questions and no one to answer them.

How long had I been here, I wondered. Was it weeks, months or years? I had no clue. I could see George coming and going from the lighthouse when I was up on the widow walk every day. The house was completely boarded up now. Had everyone forgot about me now that I was dead? Where were my parents? All these questions rambled through my mind.

Why had God not sent someone to take me to heaven? Had I been so evil in life that he would leave me here in this hell of loneliness? I had no one to talk to or, at least, no one that could hear me. One day, as I went up to the widow walk, I saw George leaving the lighthouse. I suppose he had taken on the job after both Charles and I died. As I stood there looking out at the sea, George began to make his way toward the path back to town when he stopped in his tracks and turned to look back at the house. I am not sure what caught his eye, but I could see his gaze focus on me as if he could see me. So, to test that, I waved at him. He suddenly began to stumble backwards as if he really did see me. How exciting, I thought. I think he saw me. After all this time, someone actually saw me. Of course, I was concerned for George because, honestly, I had never seen him move so quickly.

Days passed and each day, I took my trip up to the widow walk. It was all I had. My dear Charles was gone, I never had the opportunity to see my child's face, and now I was dead as well. Was I being punished for some horrible deed? And, I realized, that I did not see George.

What had happened to him, I wondered. Had I scared him so badly that he refused to return to tend the lighthouse? I sank deeper into depression. I was alone.

As I stood there, I wondered if I would ever find my way out of this house and be able to walk the cliffs near the lighthouse as I loved to do. I had never tried to leave the house. I assumed that

I couldn't, but today I was going to see if it was possible. I made my way down to the front door. I unlocked it and opened it wide. I took a deep breath and marched through the door. I did it. I am outside. I feel free.

I looked down at the pathway that led to the lighthouse, put one foot in front of the other and away I went. As I reached the lighthouse door, I noticed the lock on the door. What is going on here; why is this locked? If the lighthouse is not in operation, how are the ships making it through this passage safely? I began to panic. I did not want any woman in Dalsmith to lose a husband to the sea as I had lost Charles. What can I do, I thought? I tried to get into the lighthouse. Perhaps then I could maybe figure out a way to light the beacon again. I began to weep, thinking of how much I missed my Charles. I knew now that nothing I did would make a difference any more. There were so many things that I believed would keep me from doing anything physical. I could open doors and shutters but what good did that do. I felt so useless.

Since I could not enter the lighthouse, at least I could go out near the cliffs to enjoy the view. Standing on the cliff, I could see the town, even my parents' store. I missed everyone so much. I knew how hard my death must have been on them. I began to worry whether I would ever see them again. It really did not matter, I suppose, but I needed to know they were alright. I realized that it would not be a good idea to go into town. Since I knew George had seen me, I did not want to take a chance of scaring the life out of my parents, too. I thought it best to stay near my home where I could live out my afterlife in peace.

One day, as I stood by the cliffs, I heard the faint sound of a baby crying. Where in the world was that cry coming from? As I walked up the path to the house, I could hear it again; it seemed to be getting louder. Then I wondered who would bring a baby way out here and leave it.

I actually became quite irritated thinking of such a thing. I usually left the door open when I was outside so maybe someone had wandered inside to get out of the damp air. As I walked through the door, I noticed it was so quiet. I did not hear the baby again. I wandered from room to room, looking everywhere but found no baby.

Where is it? I found nothing, no sign of entry. What was that noise then, I wondered. That night, as I sat in my chair in my room, I began to hear a whimper or cooing like a baby would make. I actually became quite startled thinking I was being haunted. Could that baby be my own that I had lost that day? That is impossible. I lost that child after only being pregnant for three months. Something very strange is going on here. If the child is now a ghost, why could I not see it? I would love to be able to be a mother now even if I could not be one when I was alive. Again, I had so many questions and no answers. If this child could be here with me, then why is Charles not here? I thought this very odd indeed.

Chapter Four

Strange Goings On

Time passed as it always did and things at the house and lighthouse remained the same, empty and cold with me living in a nightmarish hell I was not able to understand. The baby's cries continued night after night but still I was unable to find the source. Often I walked by the cliffs just to get some relief from the sound. Was my child haunting me? Was I going mad from the guilt I felt for losing the child?

One day, as I stood on the cliffs, I saw three people walking up the path toward the lighthouse. Who is that, I wondered. As they got closer, I could see it was George and my parents. I was so happy to see someone. It had been so long. I followed them into the house. All three of them stopped as if in shock to see the front door to the house wide open. No mystery, I thought. But, of course, they did not have any idea that I was still here.

I listened to them ramble on about cleaning up the mess from months of sitting vacant.

"So who is buying the property?" George asked.

"No one. We just felt compelled to come up here to clean it up in memory of how Gwyneth would have wanted us to," my mother responded. "After all, she and Charles barely had the chance to enjoy it."

"Such a tragedy," George said, shaking his head.

"Yes, it was," my mom said. "Neither of them had the time together that their love so richly deserved. Charles adored Gwyneth, as she did him. I remember the day she came into the store after they were first married. She was so happy and was so in love with Charles she just beamed."

"Damn it, why did he have to leave her, Elaina?" my father said. "He promised her that he would never go back out to sea. Now we have lost our dear little Gwyneth. She should have never allowed him to go." George mumbled something and Mother asked what he said.

"Elaina, Patrick, you are going to think I have lost my mind with what I am about to tell you. Do you remember the day that I came up here to lock the place up and so forth?" He paused as they nodded. "As I was walking away from the house, for some reason I had an urge to look back at it."

"Go on," Mother urged.

"I swear to you that I saw Gwyneth standing up on the widow walk."

"Are you crazy?" my father blurted.

"No, I am not, Patrick. She was standing up there like she had done every day since Charles left. She smiled and waved at me."

They looked at George and then at each other before my father said, "You're serious, aren't you?"

"Yes sir, I am."

"How could that be possible?" Mother asked. "She had been dead for two months at that time."

"I understand that, but there she was as beautiful as always."

"Are you sure your eyes were not playing tricks on you?" Father asked.

"Yes, I am positive," he said.

George told his story again while I pondered how to let them know I was there. Of course, I did not want to show myself because that would be frightening. The last thing I wanted to do was to scare the life out of all three of them. As I finished that thought, I heard the sounds of the baby crying again. As I turned to again to look for the source of the sound, I glanced at my parents and George to see all three of their faces turn white.

"Did you hear a baby cry?" Mother asked the men.

"Do you see the look on our faces? Of course we did," Father said.

"Where is it coming from and how is that possible? Gwyneth's baby had not even been born yet," Mother said.

"I don't know, but I am getting out of here. This place has spooks!" George said.

"Oh don't be ridiculous, George," Father said. "It was probably just the wind or something."

"There is no wind today," Mother said.

I decided that if I wanted to get their attention, this would have to be the time, before they ran out the door screaming. So, I went over to my dining table and gave the tablecloth a little bit of a yank and off it flew onto the floor.

"Oh for goodness sake," Mother said. "Did you see that?"

"First you think we are deaf and now you think we are blind?" my father exclaimed.

"I just wanted to make sure you both saw that."

As they looked around the room, they could obviously not see me. I questioned whether I should continue, but I had been alone for so long that I needed them to know. I walked over to the cabinet with a door already slightly ajar, and gave it a shove. They looked at each other and decided they had enough of this and turned quickly to leave. My mother actually stopped, turned back toward the kitchen and said, "Is that you Gwyneth?"

I was so happy that she figured it out. "I don't hear anything," she said. "Can you do something to confirm to me that it is you?"

I quickly walked over to my rocking chair by the fireplace and made it rock back and forth.

"My dear, sweet Jesus," she said. "Gwyneth that is you, isn't it?"

"Yes, it is me," I responded, even though I knew she could not hear me. For some unexpected reason, my mother turned quickly and bolted for the door. I heard her screaming after my father and George, but they were already halfway down the path.

She did not come back that day, which I thought was odd because she now knew I was there. Oh well, I thought. Maybe they will come back some other time.

I began to get quite despondent about this whole afterlife experience. I still wondered often why Charles had not returned to the lighthouse. After all, the baby and I stayed. Maybe he did not love me at all, I thought and I became even sadder than before.

A few days later, I was up on the widow walk scanning the water as usual when I noticed my mother and two other women coming up the path. At first, I did not recognize these women until they got much closer. I realized one of them was the preacher's wife, Victoria, and the other was my mother's friend, Mary. Why are they coming up here? As they approached the house, Mary looked up at me as if she could see me standing there. I could not hear them talking from way up there, but I saw that Mary was pointing directly at me. That is interesting, I thought. I hoped that they had come to see me so I went down to find out what they wanted.

As I reached the living area, I could hear Mary telling my mother and Victoria that she felt I was standing up there so, apparently, she had not seen me. That was sad; I was hoping someone besides George would be able to see me. They all sat down around my dining room table. Victoria pulled out her Bible and told the other ladies, "It is time we bless this house to finally put Gwyneth and the child at peace" and my mother agreed and they started spouting scripture after scripture, but I did not feel any different. Was that supposed to do something?

Then they began to walk through each room of the house saying prayers and making the sign of the cross in each room as they left. I was still waiting to see or feel something different but, again, nothing happened. I appreciated the prayers, because those are always nice, but I was not really sure exactly what I was supposed to do.

"Do you feel she is still here, Elaina?" Mary asked.

"I don't know. Maybe we should try to talk to her. My dear, sweet Gwyneth, are you still here?"

I was hesitant to make any noise or move anything because I thought they had read so many nice scriptures to put me at rest that I did not want to disappoint my mother.

"Please let us know if you are still in the house," Victoria said.

Then Mary looked at them both and said she is still here and pointed in my general direction.

"Are you sure, Mary?" my mother asked.

"Yes, Elaina, she did not leave."

My mother actually broke down in tears. I suppose she was sad for me because not only was I stuck in this place but, for some reason, so was my child.

"What are we going to do now?" she asked the other ladies.

"I don't know," Mary said. "She seems very sad and confused."

Oh my goodness, I thought. She has no idea just how right she is.

Victoria started speaking directly to me. "Gwyneth, you need to go to God now. Charles is not coming back. He was lost tragically at sea, as you know. How can we help you?"

What I thought very interesting was that Mary seemed to know when I was around them. If that was true, maybe she could hear me or see me for real this time. I walked over next to her and whispered in her ear.

"Mary, I am right here."

I must have been correct because of her reaction to my whispers. Then, I leaned down and whispered again. "I don't know how to leave."

Mary stood up, looked around and said, "She just spoke to me. She said 'I am right here' and then she said 'I don't know how to leave here.'" I was not sure how she had been able to hear me when my own mother could not even manage that. So I figured maybe once more could not hurt anything. I got close to her and said, "I will be fine here. Don't worry."

She relayed my message to my mother and Victoria, adding "I don't think she is ready to leave here yet. Maybe we should come back and try this again."

My mother finally spoke up and said, "Gwyneth, I hope you can hear me, child. I love and miss you so much but it is time to leave now. You don't belong here anymore."

No one in the room knew, but I began to cry. To be honest, I was frightened to leave all that I knew. This was my home; my life was here with Charles. I thought of the day that I learned I was with child. I began to feel almost hatred for God at that moment. He had taken my husband, my child and my life. How could I ever want to go to a place where I had to leave all that I had shared with Charles? I had already done that once.

It finally seemed as if the ladies with my mother had seen and experienced all there was and wanted to return home. The last thing I heard them saying was that they would return soon to talk to me again. At least I have something to look forward to. I sat down in the chair by the front window to rest; it had been a long day.

Chapter Five

The Return

My days were consumed with searching for my child whose constant cries had become more insistent and frequent. How would I ever find my poor baby if I could not see him or her? I would love to hold my baby; it sounds so sad. Even in the afterlife, I was compelled to be a mother to my child. I hoped to find an answer to this puzzle. It had become quite the quest on a daily basis other than my usual trek to the widow walk to break up my boredom.

While making my usual stance on the widow walk that day gazing out at the sea, I tried to sort out why my daily visit seemed so important to me. I had never really pondered the reason that pulled me up there every day. I happened to glance toward the harbor, and the direction of the path that led into Dalsmith, and noticed two men. They were quite a distance away so I watched as they appeared and disappeared among the trees and twists of the path. Finally, they came out of the shadow of the tall pines that lined the cliff and I realized one of the men was George. The other man looked familiar but still I could not make out his facial features. Finally, they reached the crest of the hill below the lighthouse. The man with George wore the type of clothing a sailor might wear and he had a heavy beard. I thought I had better go down and see what they were up to; after all, this was still my home.

As I reached the living area on the first floor, I could hear George's voice outside the door so I stood near the fireplace waiting for them to enter. As the door swung open, I saw George enter first and then his companion. As the man entered, I could finally see his face clearly. I looked at his eyes, his mouth, the

150

shape of his face and I knew instantly who he was. This is not possible! Oh my God . . . it is my Charles. How? What? My thoughts were so confused at how he could not be dead? They told me he had died in the shipwreck of the Emma T.

I had to sit down; my excitement and confusion had completely drained me. Oh, my love, I thought, where have you been? And I began to weep. Suddenly, I became angry as I watched him wander around the room looking and touching everything as if he could not recall that he had belonged there before.

"Charles, we left everything just as Gwyneth had left it before her death," George said.

Charles hung his head and began to cry. "How could I have ever left her? She was my life. She did not want me to go and I promised her that I would be back. She lost her life because she mourned me. What happened to her, George? How did she die? Please tell me."

"Don't you know?" As George told my beloved how I died, he choked back tears of his own. "She miscarried your child and bled to death."

"Oh no. My poor, beautiful Gwyneth. I should have been here, George. God will never forgive me and I will go to hell for abandoning my only love."

"No, Charles, you will not go to hell. Your every intention was to come home to her. Circumstance dealt you both a harsh hand. Try to remember, my friend, that you laid in bed for many months before knowing who you were, let alone remember your life."

"Yes, I know," Charles said. "But it is still no excuse for leaving my lovely wife to be on her own in this godforsaken lighthouse. The sea is a horrible mistress to cleanse from your mind. I let her win and now I have to pay. I have lost not only the dearest women I will ever find on this earth, but I lost my child, as well. How can I ever forgive myself?"

I listened to him pronounce his sorrow over the loss of me and our child. My love for him began to swell again. Was this why I had been completely intent on gazing out to sea as if something more was to come, I wondered. I had never dreamed Charles would return. No wonder he had not returned to me in death. I spent so much time being angry at him for not being here with me. How horrible I felt at that moment.

I had to find a way to talk to him. Would he be able to accept that I am here with him? Would he hear the cries of our child as I do? I had so many questions. I heard George begin to speak as he sat down at the dining table.

"Charles, there is something I need to tell you but I can guarantee that you will not believe what I am about to say. She is still here, my friend."

"What do you mean?" Charles asked. "Of course she is still here. Her body has been laid to rest on the grounds."

George shook his head. "I don't mean that, Charles. She is still here. Her spirit haunts this house."

"Are you out of your mind?" Charles asked, chuckling.

"I am being completely honest with you, my friend. She has been seen and heard here several times by not only me, but her mother and friends, as well."

Charles didn't know how to respond and his mouth had dropped open wide. I wish I could explain the look on his face at that very moment.

"If you do not believe me now, you will. Trust me," George said. "She did not leave. I suppose she always knew that you had not died but the not knowing is what killed her."

"Your age is catching up with, my friend," Charles said.

George just shrugged his shoulders and said, "I guess you will have to find out on your own. I must go now. It is a long walk back to town and it is getting quite late."

George said goodbye and out the door he went. As Charles sat there in the silence of the home looking around, the sadness and emptiness of the house became too overwhelming I suppose because he got up and walked out the door heading for the lighthouse. I assumed that now that he had returned, he would be tending it again.

That night passed slowly as I did my best to consider how I would ever present myself in spirit to him. He spent most of the night in the lighthouse. I guessed it was because of the guilt he felt for leaving me. I had resigned myself to knowing that the happenings of the past several months had been fate stepping into our lives. There would have been nothing we could have done to change it; it was meant to be.

The only spot I could think of to do some real thinking was up on the widow walk so I made my way up there as I always did. I could see Charles scrubbing the thick glass covers that surrounded the beacon's flame. As he finished, he walked out onto the walkway at the top of the lighthouse and stood looking back at the house. Suddenly, he stood tall and, staring directly at me, he screamed, "Gwyneth!" and stumbled backwards, hitting the wall of the lighthouse.

He saw me! How wonderful. I could hear him running down the metal stairs inside the lighthouse and, soon, I saw him run out of the doorway, stop dead in his tracks and stare up at me on the widow walk. He screamed out again, "I can see you, my love!" He stood there for what seemed like several minutes looking up at me. I knew he was doing himself an injustice because I would never be able to stay with him. I knew now that I stayed because I had been waiting for him to return. I began to start feeling quite weak, almost like a shift in my very essence. I could no longer allow him to see me. His sorrow and the release of his guilt would never be complete unless I left as I was meant to and he was able to move on without me.

He ran into the house screaming my name over and over while I stood in silence watching him search each room. Suddenly, I heard our child. Charles stopped looking around. "My child!" he cried. "What is going on here?"

I felt so horrible for him and wished I could put my arms around him for comfort. I would love nothing more than to embrace him. That evening, I felt very uneasy, as if something was wrong. I sat on the end of the bed watching Charles toss and turn in his sleep. As I sat there, I heard a whimper coming from the corner of the room.

I turned to get a glimpse of a blanket lying on the floor. On that blanket, I could see a very small baby. I thought, Finally, I can see you, my dear child, and I walked over to pick it up. It was a sweet little baby girl. I wondered why my child showed itself to me now. Was it Charles that had been the key to the puzzle the whole time? Regardless, I had her now. Maybe it was a sign that my time of being stuck here was coming to a close. I sat down in the rocking chair with my darling child cuddled in my arms. I finally began to feel complete and content again. As we sat there, I starred out of the window into the darkness. I could see the moon shining upon the breaking waves on the sea. How I loved the sea. I finally understood Charles' love for it, even though it had been the one thing that had destroyed our life together.

As the sun rose, I watched Charles begin to stir. I remained still so as not to draw attention to our presence in the room. As he sat up on the side of the bed rubbing the sleep from his eyes, he gathered his thoughts and began scanning the room.

"It was all a dream," he said. "How will I ever be able to live without dear Gwyneth and my child?" After burying his head in his hands, I could see how difficult it was going to be for him to resolve our loss. I had to do something to help him. As he raised his head, I began to rock the chair back and forth so that he would know I was there with him.

He smiled broadly and asked, "Gwyneth, is that you, my love? I am so sorry my darling wife, I let you down and now you have died for my sins. Can you stay with me here?" he asked.

I was shocked that he would ask such a thing of me; did he not want me to rest in peace? I stood up with our child cradled in my arms and walked silently from the room. I could no longer watch my husband wallow in his own self pity. What had happened to him? He was always so strong. To be honest, I was disappointed that he would not think of mine and our child's best interest before his own. I wandered up the widow walk because I knew that he would not see me or hear me until he came to his senses.

After several days, I watched as he walked towards the lighthouse. Winter was beginning to rear its ugly head upon the coast.

The wind was violent that day and the waves were so large that they crashed upon the cliffs with extreme force. As the day passed, the storm gathered strength and intensity. I thought it rather odd that neither the cold nor the wind seemed to affect me or my child. It was interesting, to say the least.

I stood there watching over Charles through the windows atop the lighthouse. I could see him struggling to keep the flame lit. I knew that with the waves crashing over the lighthouse, even the inside was damp. He always kept a storage box of kerosene on the walkway so it would not be close to the flame. I saw him trying to make his way around the walk to the storage box. He reached it but when he turned, it was as if time slowed. I saw a wave strike him, pushing him over the rail. He struggled to hold on for several minutes but when the next wave came, he fell. I screamed out in horror as I watched Charles fall and land hard at the base of the lighthouse. I rushed down the stairs, put my child on the bed and ran outside to Charles.

He looked up at me and said, "You see, my dear Gwyneth. God has now made me pay for my sins of leaving you." That is all he said before he passed away. I sat there by his body for some time when I suddenly felt a tap on my shoulder. I turned to see Charles standing there.

"So, now you can see me, my love. Welcome home." We embraced one another as we did in life. We made our way back to our home. As we approached the front door, Charles said he should carry me across the threshold again.

"I don't think you can anymore, my love," I said with a laugh.

"I suppose not," he said. "Where is our child? I heard it crying last night and wanted to hold it in my arms but I could not see it."

"We have a daughter, Charles."

"Let's go get her," he said with a smile.

As we climbed to the top of the stairs, we could hear our little girl cooing. We went into the bedroom and Charles picked her up from the bed. As we stood there, we could hear the sound of the storm raging outside. Then, suddenly, there was silence.

There was no noise anymore; the silence was almost deafening. We walked to the window and looked out to see a white light that seemed to be getting closer. Charles wrapped his arms around me and our child.

"I will not allow anything to ever separate us again," he said.

"I feel this is where we are supposed to go, Charles. I now know where I was supposed to be a long time ago, but I believe God wanted me to wait for you so we could all go together as a family.

"Finally, the days on end I spent up on the widow walk was making sense to me. My attraction to the sea was me knowing that you were coming back. The cries of our child for months were also a sign and, now, so is your death It is time for us to go, my love.

"We will now be together for all eternity as it was meant to be, never to be separated again."

THE END

The Truth Shall Set You Free

By: Daniel Norvell

Chapter One

The Truth Shall Set You Free

It was a Friday night and I was working at the firehouse. I called home and spoke with my wife, telling her I would see her in the morning. I never made it home.

The shift was uneventful; we didn't turn a wheel. On the way home, I was crossing the river and on the other side of the bridge was a car accident. I stopped to help, but it was a setup. As I looked into the car for victims, a man walked out from behind the corner of a building with a gun.

"What's going on? Where are the people from this car?" I asked.

The man simply grinned at me, "There aren't any."

He lifted his gun and, in an instant, my life was over. He didn't even rob me. He just turned and walked away.

I stood there, staring at my body lying in the street in a pool of blood. The man had taken most of my face off with the gun. I sat down and thought of Mary. What would happen to my wife? What would happen to my family? An odd feeling came over me and I turned around.

There, on top of the bridge, was a light. It drew me but I never went to it. My only thought was of my wife. I ran all the way home. It seemed like minutes but, apparently, it had been hours. By the time I made it home, there were guys from the department in and out of my house, bringing food, and their wives sat with Mary, comforting her while she cried. I had never felt so bad for anyone in my life.

My funeral was huge. They carried my casket on top of the fire engine on which I served. All of the people that I worked with, in full dress uniform, walked next to the waxed and sparkling engine. The priest that delivered the sermon at my funeral gave me no comfort.

I was murdered in cold blood and there was no reason for it. I am no detective; I am a fireman. The only thing that gunman took from me was my life. I stood in the cemetery with all of the people that I held dear. I watched as the chief presented my wife with the flag that had been draped over my casket. They lowered my casket into the ground and everyone walked away. I stood alone, in that cemetery, with no answers, only questions.

I was surprised to see a beautiful woman walk up to me and say, "Alan, it is time to go."

"Who are you?" I asked.

The woman just smiled. "I was sent here to bring you home."

"You are an angel, aren't you?"

The woman nodded and looked at me sadly. "You aren't coming with me are you, Alan?"

"I can't. I can't leave my wife. I would rather sit here and keep an eye on her."

"Alan, all is not what it seems. The person you are now is being asked to come home. You are a good soul and you need to come with me. If you stay, no good will come of it."

"I'm sorry. I am staying with my wife."

Looking back on that day, I wish I had followed the angel. I would come to find out that Hell was sometimes right here on earth.

Chapter Two

Stranger Than Fiction

I went home after the meeting with the angel. Mary was sitting on the couch and I had a very funny feeling. She didn't seem the least bit upset anymore. Everyone had gone, there was just her, and she just sat there watching TV. The phone rang and Mary said to the voice on the other end, "I can meet you tonight. I'll see you soon."

I guess I was happy to see that she was not dwelling on it, but I hadn't even been in the ground for a day yet. As Mary went to get ready, there was a knock on the door. It was Joe. Mary answered the door and her entire demeanor changed in an instant.

She burst into tears and hugged Joe. "I just miss him so much, Joe. I can't bear the thought of living without him."

Joe was visibly choked up. "That kid was like my little brother and I feel a huge void every time I pass his locker. If you ever need anything, Mary, just call." And with that, Joe was gone.

Mary closed the door, her demeanor changing again in an instant. "Jackass," she said.

I was confused. What in the hell was going on with my wife? Had she snapped? Was my death too much for her to handle? I sat on the couch as Mary moved around the house, getting ready for her meeting with the voice on the other end of the phone. I decided that I would follow her to learn more.

Mary went out, started her car, and I jumped into the back seat before she left. She drove for about an hour and it was as if she was making sure she wasn't followed. She arrived at a building in the bad part of town. She got out of the car and I followed. She walked up some stairs and into the building. It was a rundown apartment building, and I could hear music playing, and kids were talking behind the various doors we passed. Mary came to a door at the end of a hallway, it was room number 223. She knocked and the door opened.

A complete feeling of dread came over me. The man that opened the door was the man that had ended my life. The door closed and Mary ran to the man and kissed him.

"How long do we have to keep up the act?" the man asked.

"Just keep your cool. As soon as the insurance pays me, I'll sell the house, his truck and everything he ever had. It will be as if he never existed."

I couldn't believe what I was witnessing. What in the hell was going on? He and Mary went into the bedroom. A few minutes later, I could hear her moaning. Clearly, I was the last thing on her mind.

I stumbled out of that apartment and all the way back to the cemetery. I stood by my grave. It hadn't even been covered for 12 hours yet. A feeling of rage came over me. I couldn't believe my wife had me killed!

I fell onto the dirt that covered my casket.

"Why? Why, Lord? I loved that girl with everything that I was. I felt like such a fool. Mary never gave any indication that she no longer loved me. I couldn't believe my entire marriage was for insurance money. I would never receive justice. I figured I was just victim of a crime that would go unsolved.

I stood over my grave for hours. Days and nights ran together and I just stood there. I never worried about anything but her for our entire marriage. Hatred and darkness filled me. I wanted justice. I heard someone walking up behind me. It was Joe. He had a bottle in his hand and he had clearly been drinking.

"I am so sorry, Al," he sobbed. "I should have taken you to breakfast that morning. Never worry, little brother. I will always make sure Mary is taken care of."

If only Joe had known. I wish I could have told him, "Joe, you are a good man. Stay away from that bitch." I wished he could hear me. Joe stumbled away, blinded by his tears, and I felt worse than ever.

I sat propped against a tree in the cemetery for days. I was looking out across the grounds and I noticed a man walking over toward me. He walked directly to me and said, "Hello, Al. Not having a very good afterlife, are you?"

"Who are you?"

"I am the answer to your prayers, Al. I am here to see that you receive justice."

I wasn't sure what to think. I was not quick to want to trust anyone.

"Are you an angel? Who sent you here?"

"I am an angel, of sorts. I am thinking that I can maybe help you find peace," he responded.

I wanted peace now more than ever, but I was not going to agree to anything.

"Nothing is free, angel. What is the price for my justice?"

"The price is not high, just your service to me after you get your justice."

"Service to you? The only being that would ask that of me is most likely not one that I would care to take up arms with. I am standing in the presence of the devil, aren't I?"

"You are," he answered with a sly smile.

"So if I promise to serve you for my justice, I spend eternity in hell?" I asked.

"Where are you now, Al? What kind of God would condemn you to the hell you suffer now?"

"I don't blame my misfortune on God. I blame it on Mary."

"Was Mary not created by the creator? Is she not a product of Him?"

"She is most likely a product of hell and manipulated by you. I don't believe people are created to be evil; I think they are convinced to be."

"You may be right, Al, but you may be wrong. I will leave you to your morality. But before I do, I will say this. A graveside vigil is not peace, either. If that's the way you wish to spend eternity while the man that killed you spends your blood money and screws your wife, then so be it. Good luck, Al. Have a nice afterlife."

As much as I hated to admit it, his words made sense. "What do I call you?" I asked.

"You can call me Mr. Black. It sometimes makes it easier for the ones that I work with to refer to me that way," he responded.

"I never agreed to work with you; I just asked your name."

"No need to get upset, Al. You may call me Mr. Black. You continue on your quest for eternity. I hope that God sends someone for you soon. But let me ask you this. Why should a man that risked his own life for strangers have died the way you did and not receive any justice for it? Think about that, Al. Think about it when winter gets here. Ghosts feel the cold, too. Death is not a release from misery."

"If I work for you, what would I have to do?"

"I knew you'd come around," he said. "It is really very simple, Al. You will be given your chance for justice and then you have to perform a task for me. After the task is performed, you will be released from anything binding. If the Lord then wants you, he can have you."

I had seen enough to realize that I couldn't let Mary and her murdering boyfriend get away with it. I wanted revenge. It made it easier to shake Mr. Black's hand. "I'll do it, but only under one condition. Mary knows it's me taking revenge for her deeds."

"Consider it my free gift to you, Al. The deal is done. You will be seen by all as mortal, but you are not. You cannot be killed, but you can feel pain. You cannot go into any church, or walk on hallowed ground, because it will destroy you. You will have certain gifts that nobody else has. You will have the ability to disappear and return here any time you feel threatened, or you have to leave a place or situation," Black said. "After your revenge is carried out, I will advise you of the task I ask of you."

Mr. Black released my hand and the smell of the fall air filled my nose and lungs. I was alive again, in a human body.

"Don't get too accustomed to it, Al. It is temporary. Once you are finished, the body I have granted to you will die. After that happens, I will return and you will be sent on your task for me."

"How long do I have?"

"You take all of the time you need, Al. I have eternity for you to pay me back. Now go. Cemeteries are not a place for those such as you. The ground will begin to burn you if you stay too long. If you need to return here, do not remain long. It will kill the body that you now have."

I hurried out of the cemetery. Mr. Black wasn't kidding; the ground was starting to burn my feet. I walked to the nearest gas station and asked to use their rest room. I entered and looked into the mirror. Mr. Black had granted me a body that looked like a body builder. I was perfect. I felt the hatred for Mary run through the blood in my veins. I would begin to figure out what I was going to do to get my revenge against her and the man that killed me.

Chapter Three

Twisted fate

The need for vengeance filled my heart. My beating heart! I was once again alive! It was a wonderful feeling to breathe air into my lungs again. I would be able to eat, to feel. I started toward home. I felt empty, but I was OK with it. I was alive! As I walked, I came closer and closer to a church. The closer I got, the weaker I felt. I had to cross the street and hurry by. Mr. Black wasn't kidding. It caused me to become weak and actually felt painful. I wouldn't make that mistake twice.

As I walked home, I passed a house where I could hear a little girl screaming. "Stop, Daddy! Stop!" I had a strange awareness. I could hear and feel the little girl's pain and anguish. I stopped and walked up to the door. I knocked but nobody answered. I could hear the little girl screaming louder. I dropped back and I kicked the door in.

I ran up the stairs and there, on the floor of a bathroom, was a man attacking his daughter. She couldn't have been more than 8 years old. I grabbed the man by the shoulder and threw him across the room without effort. He hit the wall in a hallway and got right back up. I turned and glared at him.

"You sick prick. What in the hell is wrong with you? How could you hurt your own little girl, your baby?!?"

"Who the hell are you? What gives you the right to bust into my house?"

"That little girl's screams gave me that right and, now, you are going to pay!"

The man hit me in the mouth but I barely felt it. I grabbed him by the throat and tossed him down the hall and against a door.

Beyond Life

He grabbed the handle and hurried through the door. As I made it to the room, the man had a gun pointed at me.

I put my hands up. "Calm down. You don't need your daughter to see this. I'll just leave."

The man began squeezing the trigger. The bullets passed through me and they burned. I looked down and saw no blood. There were bullet holes in the wall behind me. I looked the man in the face. "You can't kill a dead man."

"What are you?" he asked, his eyes wide with terror.

"I am the strength and revenge that your daughter does not have. I am your worst nightmare!"

A couple of more shots were fired and I heard a groan behind me. I turned in time to see the little girl crumple to the floor. The bullets had passed through me and into her.

"My God! What have I done?" the man screamed.

I knew she was dead the instant her little body hit the floor. I turned and looked back at the man. We could hear sirens. A neighbor must have called the police when the man shot at me the first time. I had to get out of here. As I started to run, I was immediately back in the cemetery. Mr. Black was standing there, at my graveside, looking at me.

"You weren't kidding. I just thought of getting out of there and I was here!"

Mr. Black back handed me and my body hit the tree behind my grave. "I did not grant you this gift to be an avenging angel. You take care of your business and that is it. I am not making deals to make you feel better."

"That little girl deserved to be protected. I tried to help her."

"It is not your concern to protect the innocent anymore. You did a bang up job, Al. She's dead. I had plans for her father and now he may repent for the sins he committed. You have probably cost me a soul. It had better not happen again or I'll return you to this grave, bind your soul inside of that shell that used to be you, and you can spend eternity in the cold ground. Are we clear?"

"We are," I responded, silently grieving for the little girl I was unable to save.

"Now get out of here. You make me sick." With that, he was gone and the burning began in my feet. I hurried out of the cemetery once again.

What a twisted fate. I am a good man, or at least I was. I feel alive, but not really. Those bullets passed through me like I wasn't even there. Flesh would have slowed them at the very least. I can't believe I could have been so stupid. I cost that innocent girl her life. The day I died, I should have just followed the angel. I could have been in the company of the Lord now and maybe I would not feel the need for revenge. Now all I have is a debt to pay to the devil, and no chance for peace. Ever.

Chapter Four

The Cost of Revenge

I knew what Mr. Black said to me was not just a threat, it was a promise. I knew my fate would be worse if I crossed him again. I decided I would take my revenge and complete my end of the bargain. After that, I would perform the task he asks and wander the earth if that would be my fate.

I decided to head for the apartment where my wife went after my funeral. I decided to repay the man that killed me. I wondered how I would take my revenge on him. I thought that maybe I would strangle him, or maybe I would throw him out his window into the street. This man had taken everything from me. He had helped Mary trick me and made me feel something real. All I could think of was killing him.

I was not sure what I was, but I knew I would have the first half of my revenge very soon. I finally made it to the apartment but the man wasn't there. I broke the door handle and went inside. I wanted him to come in and fight. He would not be able to hurt me anyway. It would be better for me if he did fight. Then I would not feel so much remorse when I took his life. I sat on the man's couch and waited for him to return. It was about three hours later when he returned home.

"Evenin', Sunshine," I said.

"Who the hell are you?"

"I am vengeance," I responded, grabbing him by the throat and lifting him at least a foot off the floor. I was amazed at my own strength. The man's eyes grew wild as I choked off his air supply. He gripped my arm with both of his hands, but his efforts were useless. The body that Mr. Black had granted me was far too strong.

As the man's eyes began to roll back into his head, I remembered that I had sworn to protect the lives and property of this city, even his. I released my grip and dropped him to the floor.

"I am a friend of the man you killed and I'm here to kill you," I said.

The man, holding his throat, spoke. "It was her idea. I didn't want to kill anybody."

"I don't believe you," I replied.

The man got up from the floor and ran into the kitchen; I followed. I was met in the kitchen by the man pointing the same gun that killed me at my face.

"Now you can find out how your friend died." The man opened fire and the bullets passed through me without any damage.

I walked up to him and grabbed the gun. He was still squeezing the trigger and I felt his arm break as I snatched the gun from him. He screamed in pain and, before I realized what I was doing, I snapped his neck like a toothpick. His lifeless body slumped to the floor.

I turned to find Mr. Black standing behind me. "Very good, Al. I wasn't sure if the revenge you felt in your heart would allow you to commit murder. I am pleased to be wrong."

"You aren't wrong. I simply reacted to being shot. Before I was aware, I snapped his neck."

"I don't care how it happened, Al. It happened. One down, and one to go."

"What about him?" I asked, nodding toward the dead man.

"I will be escorting his dark soul to hell momentarily, Al. You have the rest of the job to finish so go and finish it."

I watched as Mr. Black reached into the man's body and pulled out his soul by his hair. The man looked at me in terror. He and Mr. Black disappeared into a shadow. I wondered if that would be the way I would be taken to hell after I finished my task for Mr. Black. I heard the sound of voices heading toward the apartment. I ducked into the bathroom as police burst in.

I thought of returning to the cemetery and I was there in an instant. Night was falling as I hurried out of the cemetery. I needed to go to my house. It was time to repay Mary for her sin.

Chapter Five

Mary's Payment

As I walked toward my house, I was conflicted with feelings of revenge and remorse. I was truly sorry that I had taken the man's life. I simply reacted to him shooting at me; it was not intentional. I dropped him and I think I would have left, but he came at me shooting so I acted out of instinct.

I stopped a few blocks from my house. Was it my destiny to kill Mary?

"Now you are thinking, Al." I turned to see a young girl standing behind me.

"Who are you?" I asked.

"I am one possibility if you do not continue on the course you have set. I am yours and Mary's unborn child."

"What? Mary wasn't pregnant," I told the girl.

"Yes, she is, and even though she is a bad person, maybe the life she brings into the world will change her. Al, it is not your decision to be the judge of Mary. It is God's."

"I have made a deal with the devil. I have to hold up my end of the bargain."

"It is not just Mary that you will kill, Al. The death of the man was self-defense. This will be cold-blooded murder. You are a protector, not a murderer. Do you really think that the devil intends to make good on his end of the deal? He is a liar."

"What will happen to you without a father?"

"You are part of me. I will be strong. My mother will never speak of you, but Joe will. I will know you because of your friend. I want to know who you were by your goodness, not think that you are in peril because of the hell you suffered for revenge."

The girl was gone. I looked around in confusion. I had no place to go. I walked to a park and sat in one of the swings. I couldn't kill my own daughter. Nobody knew Mary had me killed but me.

I was just getting up from the swing when I was faced with a man in **a** white suit, bathed in a brilliant white light.

"Al, you have been deceived. You are not the man that Mr. Black has made you think you are."

"Who are you?" I asked.

"I am another angel sent for you. I am an angel strong enough to combat Mr. Black if he decides to show his cowardly face."

"What have I become? What am I?"

"You are a product of Mr. Black's quest for your soul. He is trying to prove to God that even the good souls like yours are not off limits to him."

I could not believe I had been so stupid. "What of Mary and my daughter?" I asked.

"Your love for your wife was real. Mary is mentally unstable and your friend Joe will be the protector of your daughter. He and his wife will raise her as their own. Joe loved you, Al. Do not taint all that you were by becoming what Mr. Black wants you to be."

"How do I get out of the deal I made with Mr. Black?"

"You have not yet committed a sin in the Lord's eyes. The death of the man that killed you, you have shown remorse for and he forgives you. Do not make the same mistake twice. You will not be forgiven again."

I felt sick. I was losing my strength. "What is happening?" I asked the angel.

"The body is dying, Al. You need to get to the church and get inside. It will kill the body and release your soul on sacred ground. I will be there to take you home."

I started to walk toward the church, weakening with every step. I looked up and I was on the steps of the church. I heard a voice behind me. "I will have a soul, Al. I will take the soul of your daughter!"

The angel was standing in the door of the church, his hand outstretched. "Come on, Al. He is a liar. This is the only way you will be able to protect her from him."

I reached up and grasped the angel's hand. Everything went black. I stood and looked down at the melting remains of the body that I had occupied. It became water, forming a puddle on the church steps.

"You resisted Mr. Black, Al. He will not be able to bother you anymore," the angel told me.

"What about my daughter? What will happen to her? I have made a dangerous enemy in Mr. Black."

"Your daughter will be fine," the angel assured me. "The only parents she will ever know will be Joe and his wife. Mary will be gone before your daughter is 6 months old."

"What will happen to Mary?" I asked the angel.

"Mary will end up where she belongs. She was only the vessel for your daughter, Al. She will not be around to leave any lasting impression. You daughter is the miracle of your life. She will end up being a doctor and she will be happy.

"Out of the pain that you suffered and Mary's sins, your daughter will be the good that came of it."

"What is hell, angel? Where is it?"

"Al, you were already there. I rescued your good soul from hell."

There was a bright light and I knew, then and there, that the truth had truly set me free.

THE END

A Ghost Account

By: Daniel Norvell

Chapter One

A Ghost's Account

It was a cold day in January. I remember the paramedics asking how many pills I took as I lay there on the gurney. And that siren blaring . . . blaring . . . BLARING!

The next memory I had was sitting at the dinner table with my wife. She wouldn't look at me or acknowledge my presence. She just sat there staring through me, asking why. I tried to tell her. I tried explaining that the pain was too great; that I couldn't cope without the medication the doctors had given me. I couldn't seem to take enough to numb the pain any longer. And I was getting tired of answering her and getting nothing more than a blank stare.

For at least two years, I lived in this house with her in complete silence. I tried to talk to her but she would either just walk away or go out for a drive until, one day, she didn't return. I couldn't imagine what I had done to deserve her actions.

I just sat and stared out the window. The house seemed so still. I reflected back on what it could have been that drove her from me. I stared out into the back yard on a warm summer day, when a couple of kids walked across my lawn . . . MY lawn. I hadn't mowed it in quite a while; it was long and really needed it. I yelled at them to get out of my yard but it seemed my screams fell on deaf ears. Those boys were so disrespectful. Who did they think they were?

One night as I lay in bed, wide awake, I heard a noise in the kitchen. The house was very quiet and still, as it often was lately, and I got out of bed to look around and make sure my house was secure. If those boys had returned to mess with my house for me yelling at them, well, they were gonna get an earful. How dare someone enter my house, in the middle of the night, to repay me for yelling at them.

I walked through the house and I found nothing. Nothing was there. I called out . . . to nothing. I went back to bed and I was restless. I needed my pills. Where were they? I looked all over for those pills; I couldn't find them anywhere.

"What's the use?" I remember thinking. Why did those paramedics waste their time years ago? What kind of life was I now living anyhow? I sat all day and night. I can't even remember meals or craving a drink of water. Nothing seemed to matter. But why was I destined to be stuck in the depression my wife left behind the day she drove off and left me without a word?

It was late winter when I heard the door open in the house. I walked into my living room to what appeared to be a young couple, looking toward me like I had no right in my own house. Those kids moved in without a word, just walked right in like they owned the place! When did I lose my voice? Why am I not being heard? What am I supposed to do to make these people get the message?

Chapter Two

The Next Account

How was I going to tell these kids nicely to get the hell out of my house? They moved in like I wasn't even here. They ignored everything I said and even started to rip apart my kitchen! Nights are running into days and days are running into nights.

I was so confused. I still couldn't find my pills. The last time I remember talking to anyone was a week before I went to the hospital. I spoke with my priest and explained to him that the pain in my back had become unbearable. The funny thing is that ever since the trip to the hospital, I couldn't remember any pain but I craved the pills anyway.

I often thought back to that hospital trip. Why couldn't I remember coming back home? When did a doctor release me? Why hadn't any of my friends come to visit? The only thing that gave me any solace was the radio I listened to in the middle of the night.

My wife used to get upset at me for listening to it at all hours and the new lady of the house got irritated when I listened to it. She paraded in and turned it off every time I turned it on. She reminded me of my wife and it upset me that things ended the way they did between us.

I just felt that I couldn't get my point across to anyone in the past few months. I needed to see a doctor to find out if was crazy. I saw and heard things I couldn't explain. I was having a difficult time remembering the last time I had a meal, but I never seemed to be hungry.

I wished I could return to a simpler time, when things made sense, when my wife and I could take on the world together. We built so many memories in this house. How could she just leave? Without a word, she just got up and left.

Chapter Three

I Must Be Crazy!

I was sitting in my living room staring out the window, thinking of how perfect my life once was. I heard some sort of a ruckus coming from the lady in the bedroom. She was screaming and I went to the bedroom to investigate. I took a look around the doorway and the lady of the house was sitting in a pool of blood as her husband was on the phone yelling, "Just get here . . . get here as fast as you can!"

The ambulance pulled up and they took the lady away. I'm still not sure what happened. I remember seeing her about a week later. She was sitting in the room the couple referred to as the nursery, crying. She kept a daily routine in the nursery for about a month and then the nursery disappeared under boxes and packing material.

One day, as quickly as they appeared, the young couple was gone. The house was empty and still. I couldn't believe my luck . . . they had left the radio. I turned it on and let it play for hours that night.

I remember the young couple and even though they frustrated me, I liked them. The house just seemed so empty. I remember the lady of the house cooking and singing lullabies like the ones many of my friends' wives hummed when they were expecting. I wondered where they went.

The electricity in the house went off one day and I could no longer listen to my radio. Even though I couldn't remember writing the check, I was sure I paid the electric bill. I also found it very odd that, even though it was snowing outside, I never felt cold even though the electricity had been off in the house for months. What the hell was happening?

I have felt empty and alone since the young couple moved. Once again, I was left without a word. No explanation, no thanks for letting us stay here, nothing.

Two more winters passed and then one day, there was a man standing in the doorway of my living room. He was wearing a suit and I knew he was there to cause me trouble . . . I could feel it. He looked over at me sitting on the couch the young couple had left there and he never spoke one word. He looked around as if he owned the place and this disgusting grin crossed his face. "It's perfect," he muttered under his breath.

I don't know what made me feel this way, but I had a gut feeling that this was one of the most heartless individuals I had ever seen. I actually felt uneasy and almost scared. I am not quite sure what his intent is, but I am hoping he ignores me as the young couple did. If he stays clear of me, I will stay clear of him . . . unless he takes my radio. Then we may have an issue.

Chapter Four

True Evil

It was late spring, I think, when the man in the suit moved his family into my house. It was the man, his wife and their two little kids. The little boy looked to be about 6 years old, and the little girl appeared to be about 8.

I never heard anyone but this loudmouth day in and day out. He yakked on the phone all day long and then went to work on the second shift. He returned home drunk and then I heard the smacks coming from the room that he and his wife occupied. Then he made a nightly stop in his daughter's room. Most times, he didn't come out until the morning.

There was something not right with this guy, something that made me shudder. I wanted to say something but it wasn't my place. Or was it? I mean, this was my house and they were guests here—uninvited guests.

This behavior was an everyday occurrence until one fall weekend. It was a Friday night. I remember it was Friday because I heard the loudmouth say that he had plans for the weekend. I heard him tell his wife, "You better not mess the weekend up for me or I'll beat the shit out of you, you worthless bitch."

I was so mad that I entertained the thought of hitting him. Instead, I told him to shut his mouth and not speak that way to her in my house. He ignored me, of course. The whole family did and I had become used to that treatment.

Later that night, the bastard came home and went into the bedroom he shared with his wife. I heard the smacks and I could smell the liquor on him when he walked into the house. He was a drunken mess. He was shouting and cussing and the kids were crying. I heard the lady of the house yell to him, "If you touch her again, I swear to God, I'll kill you."

His reply was, "You and whose army, you bitch. You couldn't stop a toilet from overflowing." I heard him make his way across the room as I started for the stairs. His feet were heavy and his venomous words cut into my very soul. How could a father and husband treat his wife and kids in this manner? I was going to burst into that bedroom and beat the hell out of this guy because I knew the reason for his nightly visits to his daughter's room.

As I reached for the doorknob, I heard a shot ring out; then three more. I heard one final shot as I crossed the threshold and I could hear the children screaming in their rooms. The lady had made good on her promise; she had shot him right between his eyes. She made sure he was dead by shooting him once in his crotch and twice through his chest. There was blood everywhere.

She stood there, trembling, and looked directly at me. "Who are you?" she asked.

"I am the owner of this house," I responded. I told her to put the gun down. As she dropped the gun, I saw the light behind her. The light was so brilliant and peaceful. She turned and walked into it and, as quickly as it appeared, it was gone. The only things left in that room were two bodies, the woman and her husband. The last shot I heard was the one that ended her life.

What did I just witness? How did she talk to me when she was already dead? Where were those kids? I turned and there stood the children, sobbing. My heart had never felt so heavy before or since. I felt so sorry for those children. I can't even imagine what they were feeling. I went to them and knelt down to their level.

"Don't look; it is nothing you need to see. Let's go downstairs and wait for the police," I said to coax them from the horrific scene. They turned and, without another word, we walked downstairs and waited for the police to arrive. The police called a grandmother and, for the third time in a few years, the house was empty again.

That terrible night haunted my memory every day. I couldn't close my eyes without remembering the look on that woman's face as she spoke to me for the first and last time. She was the first person that acknowledged me in years . . . and she was dead when she did it.

Chapter Five

Evil Returns

The house sat still and empty for many months. People would stop and look around at the house. I could hear bits of muffled discussion in the kitchen or the living room; then they would leave. I remember thinking that I hadn't invited these people. Why did they come to my house, walk around my kitchen and living room, and never even ask me if it was OK? I cannot believe how ignorant people can be. They came into my house, lived their lives and then, as quickly as they came, they left.

It was about nine months later when the blinds were opened and the new occupants that would share my house started moving in. They were two brothers. One had spent some time in the service and was wounded in the war. The other was a business person of some kind. I remember the soldier had terrible nightmares of his time spent in Iraq. He would wake up with cold sweats and head for the shower.

It was one night in late fall when the soldier asked his brother if he had heard or felt anything strange in the house. I had never heard anything strange in the house and I had been here for years. I could hear only bits and pieces of the conversation but it was clear the soldier was scared.

He was scared to death of the man he said he saw behind him in the mirror when he shaved. He said the man whispered into his ear at night while he tried to sleep. I remember thinking that I was the only other man in this house and I hadn't said a word to either of the brothers.

I respected the soldier for his service to our country. How he got hurt in Iraq was beyond me because that war had ended already. So who were they speaking of? I was intrigued and alarmed. I walked closer to the brothers so I could hear the conversation more clearly.

"I don't know who it is Jerry, but this fricken' guy is pissed," the solider said.

"Jack, you have been through a lot. We will call the doctor tomorrow. I promised Mom, before she died, that I would take care of you . . . and I will, little brother," the elder brother said, reassuringly.

Jack was trembling. The color drained from his face as he described the heaviness he felt in the house at night. He described the pushes he would feel as he would walk into the bedroom where "it happened."

I tried, in vain, to reassure Jack as well: "Calm down, kid. The war is over for you."

I had served in Iraq. That is where I had gotten my back injury and why the pain pills were prescribed. I knew his pain and I knew the stress and thoughts and feelings that followed when we returned home.

"That pedophile prick is here, Jerry. His wife shot him and he stayed behind," Jack told his brother.

I could see why Jack would be uncomfortable, but I hadn't seen or felt anything. I wasn't sure what Jack was talking about, but I would later find out. Over the next few months, I started to hear a familiar voice . . . the same angry voice I thought had been silenced by bullets. For God's sake, was Jack right? Was this guy still here in some form? How were we going to get him out of here? What were we going to do to keep this evil piece of garbage at bay?

It was one night in the living room and Jack had fallen into a restless sleep. I sat in the living room with him as he watched TV and finally nodded off. Then I heard it. I heard the voice of the man that had committed one of the worst acts a person could commit. I thought he had left but here he was. I could see him.

He leaned over Jack and whispered into his ear. "Soldier boy . . . soldier boy . . . SOLDIER BOY!" Jack sat up and looked around. The man was gone as quickly as he appeared. I looked at Jack and said, "I believe you now, kid."

I knew that I had, in fact, just looked at the ghost of the most evil, empty person I have ever seen. I know that whatever he is, he is now messing with this kid because he can no longer inflict physical pain on his own children.

I remember yelling out, "Leave him alone you rotten son of a bitch!" All I heard was an evil chuckle. What in the hell was going on here?

Chapter Six

Evil Makes His Move

Jack was at the end of his rope. This guy took joy in really making Jack's life miserable. I had only seen him once, but that was all it took for me to believe Jack.

Jerry called the doctor one night while I listened in the kitchen. He thought Jack was suffering from something they call PTSD. I wasn't sure what it was, but I was sure Jack suffered from the continuous tirade of crap this guy whispered into his ear every night. I stood in Jack's room every night and watched. I watched him sleep. When he slept on the couch, the man started his abuse. When he slept in his room, the man started his abuse. It was really starting to piss me off. This kid served God and country and this baby-raping garbage heap found pleasure in elevating his pain.

Jack was driven to the brink the second time I saw the man. Jack locked himself in the bathroom and Jerry called the ambulance. Jack was screaming, "Stay out of my head!"

I felt so sorry for this kid because he was helpless. I felt helpless, too. How do you fight what you can't see? By the time the paramedics arrived, Jack's wailing had stopped. Jerry and the paramedics pushed the door open to find Jack on the floor in a growing pool of blood. Jack had taken a razor and slit his wrists so deep that I thought he had died for sure. The paramedics rushed him out of the house while I stood in the bathroom in shock.

I thought of all of the tragedy this house had seen over the years and how much of it I had observed with my own eyes. As I stood there, I noticed the fogged mirror. On it was written, "Soldier boy Jack, why did you ever come back?"

I shouted out, "Why don't you try that shit with me, you dark son of a bitch!" I punched the mirror as hard as I could. I punched that mirror at least five times but the message was still there, fading only as the cool air filled the bathroom. I caught a glimpse of a shadow standing behind the shower curtain and then it was gone.

Jack was gone for weeks. I missed that kid. He was a kindred spirit . . . a soldier. He reminded me of myself. I sat in the living room and watched out the window. Every time the car pulled up, I expected Jerry to help Jack into the house. It never happened.

One night, Jerry came home and started packing Jack's things. I later heard him on the phone thanking the doctor for everything he had done. The last thing Jerry packed into the box was a picture of Jack in his uniform.

"I am so sorry Jack. I failed you. And Mom, I failed you, too!" Jerry sobbed loudly into his hands, falling to his knees. I asked Jerry what happened and he didn't answer. My worst feelings were confirmed a few days later when Jerry carried in the flag that had been draped over his little brother's casket.

The thing was, the whole time Jack was gone, I never heard or saw anything in the house. I looked every night for that sick bastard and never found him. He never made himself known to anyone but Jack and I. Now Jack was gone and I knew this man was responsible in some way.

About a month later, an event I had become used to came to pass once more. The boxes came in. Jerry packed them up and moved away. I never saw him again. I missed Jerry and Jack and I felt terrible for that kid. I walked into the room Jack had stayed in while he lived here and for the first time in years, I dropped to my knees and prayed. I prayed Jack would find peace and I prayed that if hell existed, the man in the suit would be condemned to it.

Chapter Seven

The End of Innocence

It was late summer. A few months after Jerry left my house, the most angelic little girl I had ever seen moved in with her parents. I saw her walk up the sidewalk outside and heard her little voice as she said, "Mommy, is this my room?" I cringed with fear. I told the little girl's mommy that maybe that would not be a good room for her, but she just gave me the same blank stare that I always got.

A month after they settled in, the torture of this little girl began. It began as the boogie man in the closet story. The little girl would run into her parents' room and they would tell her there's no such thing as ghosts or a boogie man. I remember thinking they were right; this man was worse.

The little girl became the object of the man's twisted desires. She woke up crying every night. I finally got so sick of it that, one day while the family was gone, I walked around the house screaming at the top of my lungs: "Why? Why don't you go and rot in hell? It wasn't enough that you tortured your own child and Jack. I hope that hell has a burner for your ass, you sick son of a bitch!" I never got a response.

I finally started sleeping in little Shelly's room every night. I never saw or heard anything. I watched her until she woke up screaming. I was never aware of any presence. One morning, Shelly woke up with scratch marks all over her stomach.

Her mother was horrified. She asked what had happened and Shelly said the boogie man was touching her.

I was beyond pissed. I planned to make it my mission to banish this sick bastard to hell. I prayed to God every night to give me one shot at this prick. I prayed that God would give me the ability to hog tie this guy and throw him into the pit of hell.

One night, I lay in the living room looking out the window, thinking of the hell I've endured watching the suffering in this house. I was just about to walk upstairs when I heard Shelly's terrified scream.

I charged up the stairs, two at a time, and into her room. I saw that beautiful little face with three deep scratches across it. I was at my wit's end. "That's it!" I shouted. "Where are you? Where are you, you cowardly baby raper? Why don't you come face me?"

I got my wish. There he was, standing in Shelly's closet, the bullet hole between his eyes. "I have heard you all the time. I just refuse to listen to a reject," he muttered.

I walked up to him and said, "Death was too good for you, you sick bastard! Why don't you go to hell where the pieces of shit like you should be flushed!"

"You haven't got the balls for it," he replied with a cold smile. He backed into the closet and disappeared. I ran into the closet and pounded on the wall.

"They should have ground your nuts in a blender before they buried you, you sick prick! You stay away from that girl! You stay away from Shelly!"

After that confrontation, things were quiet for around a month. That is when Paige came into the picture. Paige was the family's answer to the attacks on Shelly. Paige proved to be a guardian angel sent from above for both Shelly and I.

Chapter Eight

The Battle Begins

Paige came into Shelly's room and introduced herself. "I'm Paige and I am going to make the boogie man go away."

Shelly got off of her bed and hugged Paige with tears streaming down her face. "Thank you," she whispered.

Paige asked Shelly to leave the room and go downstairs with her mother and father. As Shelly obeyed, Paige looked directly at me and said, "I know you are here and I know that you are watching over Shelly."

"Yes. Yes, I am. But how do you know?" I asked.

"I can hear you and I can feel you, but I cannot see you," Paige replied.

Was she blind? I was standing not two feet in front of her.

"What's your name?" she asked.

"Michael. Michael Warren," I replied.

"Well Michael, it is nice to meet you. Can you tell me what is going on here?"

I described every incident to Paige in detail. She sat on Shelly's bed and nodded.

"You told him they should have ground his balls? Nice," she said with a little giggle. "He is a negative entity, Michael; a very nasty character. We need to get rid of him. Will you help me?"

I told her I would be thrilled to help her get this nasty bastard out of these people's lives and out of my house. Paige advised me to be ready; we would make our move tomorrow night.

Paige stayed the night with Shelly in her bed. I kept watch at the foot of the bed with my eyes never leaving the closet door. If this bastard was going to show himself, I would be ready. He didn't show up that night.

Paige returned to Shelly's room after breakfast and lit some sage. She said it would weaken the man to allow her to bind him and exile him to Hell or wherever the Lord decides to send him. I cannot explain it, but I trusted and believed her.

Later that afternoon, Paige walked into the room and called, "Michael, are you here with me?"

"Yes, I'm here. Are we still going to get this guy out of here tonight?"

Paige said we were. "Michael, I need you to focus. Focus all of your energy. When you do, I want you to grab the man and I want you to push him into the portal I am going to open."

I asked her how. "Michael, are you faithful?" she asked. I said I was.

"Michael, you have more strength than you know," she responded. "You will be able to grab him and push him through. You will be the eyes that I do not have."

I agreed and steeled myself to do battle with a ghost, a ghost determined to make everyone he came in contact with miserable. He hadn't done anything to me personally except insult me, but the torture he put this little girl through, and the murder of Jack, was enough for me. I was ready.

Chapter Nine

War!

Night fell and the house was still. Paige had Shelly go downstairs with her parents. She gave Shelly's parents a golden cross and a bottle of holy water. She said some blessings and told them not to fear.

Paige returned to Shelly's room and called to me.

"I'm here," I responded.

Paige repeated that my faith will be my strength and that I was the key to success this night. We began with a prayer that Paige said aloud to protect us. She then lit some more sage and moved about the room. She had holy water, sea salt and sage and a whole bag of tricks that she carried with her. I was just going to ask Paige if she thought the man had left when the closet door flew open and out he came.

As I inspected him a little more closely, I could still see the bullet hole between his eyes; or rather between the two empty, black holes where his eyes should have been. I waited for the signal from Paige.

She was finishing a prayer as he moved between us. He didn't speak as he moved silently toward Paige.

"Now, Michael!" Paige screamed. Grabbing to cover the man's face, I shoved him back into the closet. I pushed harder than I have ever pushed before.

"Michael, get out of there now," Paige yelled. I stumbled backwards as I saw something surround the man and then he was gone. The house actually felt lighter.

"He's gone," Paige said, simply. "How about you, Michael? When are YOU going to cross?"

Chapter Ten

When Will I Go Home

I walked over to Paige and looked her in the eyes. She was staring into space.

"What did you just ask me?" I said.

"I asked you when are you going to cross over?"

"What do you mean?" I asked, my confusion growing.

Paige continued asking questions: When was the last time I had a real conversation with another person? When was the last time I left the house? When was the last time I ate?

I couldn't answer her because I honestly couldn't remember. The days and nights seemed to run together and it seemed like months passed in the blink of an eye.

Paige explained that she had looked up the history of the occupants of this house. She said that Michael Warren had died of a drug overdose from prescription medications years ago. I was in awe; I told her there must be some mistake. I didn't kill myself. She said she knew I didn't do it intentionally but I didn't survive the overdose, dying on the way to the hospital.

My God! No wonder my wife wouldn't speak to me. It all started to make sense. I asked her many questions. She said my wife was fine, although she never remarried.

She said Jack died in the hospital. The man followed him there, not leaving him until Jack finished what he had started.

"Michael, it is time to go. Time for you to move on and find peace," Paige said, softly.

"I can't move on! What if the man returns? What if he attacks Shelly again?"

"Michael, your battle is over. You have fulfilled your duty. The Lord wants you to come home, but the decision is yours." Paige advised me that I would not see her again, unless the Lord willed it, and she hoped I would consider what we had talked about. Paige asked me to join her in saying the Lord's Prayer and she was gone.

When she moved into the house, Shelly was a 5-year-old girl. I remained by her side in the house until, one day, I heard, "It's time to go. You don't want to be late for your own wedding, Shelly!"

I stayed at her side, ever vigilant, a spiritual sentinel, if you will, until it was another man's duty to stand by her.

The next few years were empty. Seasons came and went in the blink of an eye. I often wondered what Paige meant when she told me the decision to cross would be mine. With Shelly gone, I had no reason to stay. So why was I? I prayed, "Lord Jesus, bring me home to heaven." I looked around and found nothing more than the same walls.

A few years later, Shelly's parents left my house. The house became silent and still and fell into disrepair. Kids would come into the house. I would watch them to make sure that they didn't get hurt. But, what would I do if they did get hurt? It wasn't like I could call an ambulance.

One night, I was standing upstairs in the bedroom where I spent my last night among the living. I reflected on the events of that night and the events that had taken place in this house over the years. I asked aloud," Lord, why I am still here? Why have you forsaken me?" No answer came.

Months passed and, one autumn night, there came a knock at my door. Although I didn't answer it, I heard the door open and close. I then heard a voice I hadn't heard in years.

"Michael? Michael, are you here?" I got up from the floor and walked down the stairs to find a soldier in full dress uniform.

"Michael, I was sent here for you. I was sent by the Lord to bring you home," Jack told me.

"My God! Jack! You can see me?! You can hear me?"

"Michael, I heard you the night you told the voices to leave me alone. I heard you every time you tried to confront the man. I have never forgotten you."

I hugged him. "Damn man, it is so good to see you! I can't leave. What if the man returns? What if he returns for Shelly or Paige?"

"Michael, Paige is the one that sent me. She wanted me to let you know she loves you and she is grateful she got the chance to meet you . . . to meet her daddy."

"Her daddy?" I asked, incredulously. "Jack, I have no daughter. Megan and I couldn't have kids. We tried. We wanted them, but we never had any."

"The night you died, Megan had planned a dinner date with you and was going to tell you she was pregnant. She never got the chance."

"Jack . . . Megan was here for years! I would have seen a baby."

Jack explained to me that I saw what I wanted to see of Megan. In reality, Megan moved in with my mother a week after I died. She had Paige and lived out her life caring for our daughter, never to marry again. I felt so sorry for **her**. Why did she not move on?

"Jack, why you? Why were you sent for me?"

"They sent me, Michael, because I was the first one that you were willing to sacrifice yourself for without question. They sent me because we are kindred spirits. There are no coincidences, Michael. It's time to go."

"I have to see Paige one more time, Jack. I have to see my little girl. I can't go with you. I'm sorry."

"Michael, Paige sent me. You will see her. We have to make a stop first and then you will see Paige," Jack said.

For the first time in decades, I left my house. I followed Jack out the door, across the lawn, and ended up in a hospital. We were standing in a room and things were unclear. I could hear a voice over a baby crying. I walked closer to the bed and Paige was sitting next to it holding the hand of her daughter—and her new granddaughter.

Paige turned, looked toward me, and said, "Thank you for coming to see what you created, Daddy."

"I love you. I am sorry." I hadn't seen Paige in years; my God, years!

"Daddy, it is time to go with Jack. It is time for you to go be with Mom and Grandma. I will be with you again, I promise."

Jack took me by the hand, and said, "It's time, Michael."

At that, I heard a voice behind me . . . it was Megan. She waited in the light to meet Jack and me. It had finally come for me.

THE END